Milton's Poetry
of Independence

Oliver Cromwell Visits John Milton
by David Neal, 1885
(courtesy of the Milton S. Eisenhower Library of the
Johns Hopkins University)

> . . . peace hath her victories
> No less renown'd then warr, new foes arise
> Threatning to bind our souls with secular chains:
> Help us to save free Conscience from the paw
> Of hireling wolves whose Gospell is their maw.

Sonnet 16

Milton's Poetry
of Independence

Five Studies

George H. McLoone

Lewisburg
Bucknell University Press
London: Associated University Presses

Associated University Presses
440 Forsgate Drive
Cranbury, NJ 08512

Associated University Presses
16 Barter Street
London WC1A 2AH, England

Associated University Presses
P.O. Box 338, Port Credit
Mississauga, Ontario
Canada L5G 4L8

The paper used in this publication meets the requiremts
of the American National Standard for Permanence of Paper
for Printed Library Materials Z39.48-1984.

Library of Congress Cataloging-in-Publication Data

McLoone, George H., 1945–
    Milton's poetry of independence : five studies / George H.
McLoone.
        p.   cm.
    Includes bibliographical references and index.
    ISBN 0-8387-5403-1 (alk. paper)
    1. Milton, John, 1608–1674—Religion. 2. Christian poetry,
English—Puritan authors—History and criticism. 3. Christianity
and literature—England—History—17th century. 4. Dissenters,
McReligious—England—History—17th century. 5. Puritans—England-
-Intellectual life. 6. Puritan movements in literature.
7. Protestantism and literature. I. Title.
PR3592.R4M35   1999
821'.4—dc21   98-33975
                                                                        CIP

To family, friends, and colleagues

Contents

Preface

The following studies examine patterns of ecclesiological and affective imagery in Milton's *Lycidas*, the Twenty-Third Sonnet, and the last books of *Paradise Lost*, *Paradise Regain'd*, and *Samson Agonistes*. The essays attempt close readings of the poems while at the same time they adhere to a historicist view that Milton's ecclesiastical nonconformity, his Puritan Independency, had important uses in his poetic art. Both general and specifically topical kinds of religious independence are hardly new subjects in Milton scholarship, especially in commentaries on his prose, but images of independence in Milton's poetry, I believe, have yet to be sufficiently explored. The five studies here are steps in that direction, I hope, but the book as a whole does not pretend to survey all the lights and shadows of Puritanism reflected in the poems or to interpret fully their wonderfully complex psychologies of love, sin, and guilt. If the book does have a larger critical purpose, it is simply to appreciate a great poet's depictions of keen and heroic minds struggling for independence from establishmentarian frames for identity.

Milton's ecclesiology and theology, or at least their tendencies, can be garnered from prose works (such as the antiprelatical tracts) undoubtedly written by him. The more systematic primary source of Nonconformist Protestantism listed in the Milton canon by the majority of Milton scholars is the treatise, *De Doctrina Christiana*, discovered among his state papers in 1823. I cite a number of passages from *De Doctrina* here, but I have tried to avoid letting the argument rest on this work alone.[1] Among the many excellent secondary sources on Milton's Protestantism and its climate, I have found *Milton in the Puritan Revolution* by Don M. Wolfe (1941), *Milton and the Kingdoms of God* by Michael Fixler (1964), *Milton and the English Revolution* by Christopher Hill (1977), and Ernest Sirluck's book-length introduction to vol. 2 of *The Complete Prose Works of John Milton* (1959) consistently useful and thought-provoking. Criticism on Milton's poetry that is of a more specific kind will be cited throughout.

Unless otherwise indicated, quotations from Milton's poetry are taken from *The Complete Poetry of John Milton*, ed. John T. Shawcross (New York: Anchor, 1971). Quotations from Milton's prose are from *The Complete Prose Works of John Milton*, general ed. Don M. Wolfe (New Haven: Yale University Press, 1953–82), abbreviated as Yale Prose.

Somewhat different versions of the essays on *Lycidas*, the Twenty-Third Sonnet, and *Samson Agonistes* have appeared in *Milton Studies*, *The Milton Quarterly*, and *Mosaic: A Journal for the Interdisciplinary Study of Literature*, respectively.[2] I would like to thank the editors of these journals for their advice on preparing the earlier versions, and for permission to publish the essays here. I would also like to thank Greg Clingham and his associates at Bucknell University Press for their comments on the whole manuscript, and my daughter, Suzette McLoone, for her help in preparing the manuscript for the press.

Milton's Poetry
of Independence

Introduction

Milton's ecclesiology, we know from his prose writings, evolved into some kind of Puritan Independency. We do not know, however, Milton's own practice of worship in his maturity, or whether he belonged to any Nonconformist or Independent congregation, or to what extent he may have finally separated not only from the Anglican communion but also from the visible church militant of other Puritans. In his polemical tracts, other than the *First Defense*, he uses the terms "Puritans" and "Independents" rarely, "Nonconformists" and "Separatists" even less, and he seems reluctant to identify himself with a particular group or sect of radical Protestants. "Reformed Churches" and "Protestants" are his more frequent terms in contexts that nonetheless repudiate the less-radical Protestantism of Anglican episcopacy and Presbyterianism. Most biographers describe him as following the kind of Independency associated with Cromwell during the Civil War and the Commonwealth, although the boundaries of this nonconformity were themselves fairly elastic once Anglican prelacy had been rejected. In the *First Defense*, Milton defines Independents, in response to Salmasius's cabalistic depiction of them, as "those who refuse to recognize any orders or synods as higher than the individual churches, and who feel as you do that all such should be uprooted as offshoots of the hierarchy or rather its very stem. For this belief they are called Independents by the ignorant." He praises the Independents for refusing (unlike the Presbyterians) to compromise with a tyrannical monarch, Charles I. For Milton, Independents remained the only consistent opponents of the king, and, perhaps more importantly, they knew "how to be true to themselves until the end and how to use their victory" over the king and the established church; i.e., they were suited to lead the nation. In the *Second Defense*, he credits their victory not simply to military tactics and strategy but to the prior traits of virtue and wisdom needed to ensure a viable leadership for England. Of course, he was painfully disillusioned about the prevailing virtue and wisdom even among many Independents at the time of the Restoration.[1]

Like the term "Puritan," "Independent" in Royalist and Presbyterian contexts was used to stigmatize a variety of Nonconformists whose ecclesiologies ranged from the "Individualism" of the Seekers and the "Absolute Voluntarists" to the newly established church of Cromwell's Protectorate. Thomas Goodwin, for instance, who was known to Milton during his Cambridge years and served with Milton as an employee of the Council of State, was an Independent associated with the Protectorate's national, if also congregational, church. In the Westminster Assembly of Divines, he had been one of the few "dissenting brethren" opposed to the dominance of the Presbyterians. Roger Williams, whom Milton probably also knew, was considered a more radical Independent or Individualist after turning away from an establishmentarian kind of congregationalism— the New England–model theocracy then influencing the Protectorate.[2]

To Royalist Anglicans, Independency was nearly synonymous with anarchy. To Presbyterians, it seemed frustratingly and dangerously protean. To its adherents, it was an inspired and dynamic concept of the essential church. Although the essential nonconformity of Independency is clear enough, in his *Dissuasive From the Errours of the Time* (1645) the Presbyterian Robert Baillie complains of the difficulty he has pinning down Independents in the assembly, a complaint aggravated by "their principle of mutabilitie, whereby they professe their readiness to change any of their present Tenets."[3] Like Milton by the time of *Areopagitica* (1644), Independents became increasingly uncomfortable with Presbyterian authority. The famous Independent clergyman, Henry Burton, whose publications and public suffering must have been known to Milton, took significant issue with the Presbyterian form of church government as well as with prelatical Anglicanism. In *A Vindication of Churches Commonly Called Independent* (1644), he refutes his "late companion in tribulation," the Presbyterian William Prynne who had published an "unmasking" of Independency. Both Burton and Prynne had suffered the pillory and prison for their attacks on prelacy, but now Burton as an Independent would declare their differences. Independents do not "glory in this name," he argues, yet "are not so ashamed of it, as utterly to disclaime it." The name not only serves to set them off from Presbyterians but also "to signifie that we hold all particular Churches of Christ, to bee of equall authority, . . . that each Church is under Christs government, as the sole head, King, Lord, Law-giver thereof."[4]

Both Milton and Burton were attacked by Joseph Hall for holding the Independent view that congregations might elect their own ministers. Indeed, as Don M. Wolfe has noted, Hall's response to Burton's tract, *Protestation Protested* (1641), seems to have bolstered Milton's own Independency.[5] Like Milton, Burton regarded his reading public as in dire need of hearing the Reformation's good news of Christian liberty: Cut off from true witness and fair debate, the misinformed English people are still influenced by privilege and by money in politics and religion. Both Milton and Burton feared widening the franchise to such an electorate, one still tending to vote for the king and his party and, in Burton's phrase, "against Christ."[6] For Burton, Independency is part of the same historical occasion as that of Milton's uncloistered virtue in *Areopagitica*—the need for a Reformation of Christian minds as well as of the English church. "For *England* is generally ignorant of the mysterie of Christs Kingdome," Burton states prophetically in his *Vindication;* "the *Prelates* usurped all, suppressed altogether this Spirituall kingdom; no ministers durst so much as mutter a word of it." Prelatical tyranny has resulted in a confused, wayward Reformation in England, with few Christians prepared for God's kingdom, few now wearing "the Wedding garment."[7] In its ecclesiology and doctrine, Burton's Independency emphasizes the Communion of Saints as ruled spiritually by Christ, "the full and sole King, reigning in the heart and conscience of every true beleever." At the same time, the essential church is also a "spirituall Republick," where even Milton's views on divorce can receive a fair hearing.[8]

A sense of Independency, if not always the term itself, suffuses Milton's prose writings, and the *First Defense* is but one of many instances in which he indicates his hostility to the established church. This context and others, however, also imply a more positive Reformation ideal, one transcending political disillusionment. It is that of restoring a Pauline ecclesiology to the minds of the faithful, a concept and figure of the essential church as a body independent of secular and geographic prerogatives. An ideal vehicle for conveying truth, charity, and salvation, the "invisible church" of Reformation ecclesiology is potentially a state of mind and spirit continuous with the mystical body linking Christ and believers, a state complemented by visible congregations, reformers hoped, but not ultimately dependent on them. For Puritans, the "visible" church (the term used in the Articles of

Religion in the *Book of Common Prayer*) was a mixed community of saints, sinners, and hypocrites. The "invisible" church (a Calvinist and Lutheran term derived from Augustine) was, of course, pure. Most Puritans encouraged church membership in right-minded congregations, if not in the established Anglican Church, but many would allow with Calvin for salvation outside the church within temples of one believer.[9] Milton may have found breathing room and inspiration in this doctrine.[10] The rhetoric that justifies reforming the body of the church, what Michael Lieb has called the "organicist polemic" in Milton's prose tracts, can also be heard in the poetry, especially where images of the pastoral and marital body suggest Congregational ideals. The image of the church as used in the poetry, as these studies will try to demonstrate, can be a complex symbol rather than a simply corporal allegory, and can function expressively, taking on the affective charges of a complex psychology of religion.

Milton, of course, remained on the field of polemical controversy until the end of his life. But, as Michael Fixler has reminded us, he "never forgot that his first calling was as a poet." Further, in sustaining the Puritan aims of righteousness and God's glory, "poetry was at least equal to the Church as an instrument of Grace."[11] As if derived from the Independents' supposed "principle of mutabilitie," Milton's concept of the church as Christ's kingdom lacked explicit covenants.[12] To be sure, the visible church for Milton was a valid frame for worship, if also a dispensable one. But, "the deepest fellowship was that of the Invisible Church," and its "timeless universalism." The evolution of Milton's ecclesiology, Fixler rightly observes, is in this direction, which is at the same time "an emphasis on inward illumination and the independent responsibility for righteousness regardless of outward circumstances."[13] Here "independence"—in lowercase—implies Christian liberty as it was understood by Milton: "that election meant freedom, that freedom meant choice, and that choice meant the confirmation visibly of the righteousness innate within the regenerate." Visible confirmation, however, might well be more humanistic than strictly ecclesiastical. Eventually, for Milton the kingdom of Christ as a church is the Paradise within, an inner kingdom of conscience, and, as Fixler points out, "the change was crucial."[14] This attitude is summarized in *A Treatise of Civil Power in Ecclesiastical Causes* (1659): "The whole matter of religion under the gospel" is no more than "faith and charitie; or beleef and practice," which flow from "faculties of the inward man" as nurtured by God's grace, scripture, and "common sense." Like one's inward faculties generally, religion cannot be forced. Christ himself "rejects outward force in the government of his church" in order to better "shew us the divine excellence of his spiritual kingdom" and its superiority to earthly kingdoms (Yale Prose, 7:255–56). Such is the doctrine and practice Michael recommends to Adam at the end of *Paradise Lost*, the legacy of "A Paradise within thee, happier farr" than exalted, earthly places (*P.L.,* XII.586–87), and which Jesus recovers for all the faithful in *Paradise Regain'd*.

The subjective Christianity of Independency (and of independent-minded believers in the broadest sense) can also be a crucial Paradise, a complex theater of choice and confirmation. Here the church can be a realm of truth and congregational assurance but also a place of seeming alienation and leveling reminders of the heritage of sin. The independent consciousness repudiates establishmentarianism (or perhaps "deconstructs" it) in its witness only to confront the hierarchic impulses of an otherwise creative ego. In more specifically literary terms, Milton's Independency is perhaps relatable to his resistance to allegorical reductionism in the relationship implied between his poetic voice and his readers. This amounts to an edifying "challenge" to readers once complacently Royalist in their attitudes of historic interpretation, as Sharon Achinstein has observed, an intentionally redemptive ambiguity in parts of *Paradise Lost* leading "readers down a path toward spiritual enlightenment that involves learning how to read."[15] Here we might note Marvell's similarly independent (if not Independent) dynamic in his Cromwell ode, as the informing irony of a lyricist reacts to the state drama of the king's execution and the rise of the lord protector. Marvell's lyric speaker seems to contest with his own presumptions while depicting two minds of the people regarding the king as tyrant and martyr and Cromwell as crusader and opportunist. This cautionary anxiety consistently undermines his praise of the protector's generalship. Images of statecraft and strategy at first seem to enhance some prior design for the great national drama but are then nearly overwhelmed by an affective, spontaneous intuition:

> What Field of all the Civil Wars
> Where his were not the deepest Scars?
> And *Hampton* shows what part
> He had of wiser Art:
> Where, twining subtile fears with hope,
> He wove a Net of such scope,
> That *Charles* himself might chase
> To *Caresbrooks* narrow case:
> That thence the *Royal Actor* born

> The *Tragick Scaffold* might adorn:
> While round the armed Bands
> Did clap their bloody hands.
> *He* nothing common did, or mean,
> Upon the memorable Scene:
> But with his keener Eye
> The Axes edge did try:
> Nor call'd the *Gods* with vulgar spight
> To vindicate his helpless Right,
> But bow'd his comely head
> Down as upon a Bed.
> This was that memorable Hour
> Which first assur'd the forced Pow'r.[16]

The somewhat sarcastic reference to Charles's histrionic public relations develops into actual praise of the king's deportment on the scaffold. The "memorable Hour" of this occasional poem escapes its political framework; the tragic scene eludes aesthetic and cultural simplification by its affective complexity. The memorable event itself had also gotten away from Cromwell's "wiser Art," provoking sympathy for the king and perhaps hostility against the military. Praise for the general continues in the ode, but in the dramatically worrisome terms of *Fortuna* and her consequent cycle of potentially tragic *de casibus* tales. Conspicuously, Cromwell is called "the Wars and Fortune's Son," and his authority would seem to rely on sublunary might. His erect sword can "fright / The Spirits of the shady Night" (a fiendish alliance of political instability, superstition, and royal martyrology), but, unsettlingly, "The same *Arts* that did *gain* / A *Pow'r* must it maintain" (lines 113–20). As Commonwealth readers, we might expect some direct allusion to a larger, Christian context of history, but instead we hear the poet witnessing shadows of deliverance, theaters of otherwise necessary historical episodes whose providential sanction seems temporary, and which are unstable in their hierarchic significance for the true believer. This lyric voice, too, levels the field of civil contest, freeing the careful reader's mind from establishmentarian identity while it authorizes a repentant moral psychology, a state of mind in which truth fairly and openly confronts error past and present. The Independent consciousness affecting Milton's poetry, I believe, is even more provocative and ministerial.

The first study in this collection, on *Lycidas*, regards the body of the

drowned shepherd as the central figure of the poem, one that is simultaneously invisible and imagined and that functions as a lyric symbol of the
crisis of identify as well as an allusion to the essential identity of the church.
The quest for a redemptively spousal figure, one able to convey truth and
forgiveness, also influences the psychology of guilt experienced by the
grieving husband of the Twenty-Third Sonnet, as discussed in the second
study. A hero's knowledge of how to be true to the self "until the end" and
of how to use the victory over sin and temptation is a theme explored in the
studies of *Paradise Lost*, *Paradise Regain'd*, and *Samson Agonistes*. Over-
coming both establishmentarian and egoistic tendencies in the course of
right worship is a significantly epic task for Adam and Eve in the denouement of *Paradise Lost*. In *Paradise Regain'd*, one measure of the Son's
heroism is that he engenders an abiding figure of victorious knowledge for
all humankind, an essential church or ecclesiology that is an analogue of
Independency. In *Samson Agonistes*, the failure of statist heroism to engender analogues of timeless devotion and unlocalized celebration suggests the weakness of a spiritual independence lacking charity.

In Philistine Gaza, and in Milton's epic places of heaven, hell, and the
garden, the freedom to worship prophetically and to question authority can
lead to will-worship and self-serving mythology when charity and forgiveness are obscured by pride. This same freedom can also lead to truth, to
salvation, and to the Father's greater glory. The characteristics found in a
rightly informed Independency, its dialectical and interpretive freedoms,
are encouraged by God the Father and discouraged by Satan, who merely
seems to open the mind to truth. The Son in *Paradise Lost* arrives at the
truth of his heroic identity as incarnate Redeemer by means of prophetic
dialogue with the Father, perhaps a kind of disputation (bk. III). Adam
engages the Father in a dialogue about gaining an appropriate mate and
partner (bk. VIII). In the episode of the fall (bk. IX), Eve and Adam obscure prophetic insight and the Father's will with egoism and carnal worship, as they dispute, separate, and succumb to the Tempter. In the story of
all things that is the epic, however, both inspired and hazardous independence prove crucial in salvation history and in the completing of human
identity—man and woman free to err, repentant, then restored to communion with each other and with the Son and Father. In *Paradise Regain'd*, the
incarnate Son stands on the temple of his ancestral, established religion,
now superior to the structure of the old law, in opposition to Satan and to a
secularism threatening the body and clouding the mind. He is a sufficiently

standing congregation of one, and then one with the angelic choir; in time, he will be one with his disciples, a figure of the mystical body linking the congregations of heaven and earth.

For Milton, the heritage of temptation and sin acknowledged in the Son's encounter with Satan and contextualized for use in a ministry of the word is essential knowledge for right-minded congregations and for the individual Christian hoping to lead a sanctified life. This "warfaring Christian" (the literate Christian of *Areopagitica*), like the Son, is confident that truth will ultimately prevail in a combat with error and illusion. Independency encourages reformed Christians to recognize and confront the heritage of temptation militantly, fortified by the ministry of the word. Established religion, weakened by its appetite for civil power, fails Christians when it obscures images of fallibility with mythography and ritual, narrative ceremonies subordinating the great cause of repentance to the desire for fame. In *Lycidas*, the drowned body of Christ's minister, a complex image of sin, corruption, and salvation, is at first enclosed and obscured by a mythographic pastoralism, an establishmentarian ceremony. The corporal figure is saved, as it were, from this weak context of fruitless grief and selfish fear by the elegist's reformed, maturing consciousness of a transcendent congregation, a state of mind regarding the absent shepherd as a spiritually dynamic presence and an occasion for prophetic witness. The "uncouth swain," in his variously interrogating modes of lament, introspection, prophetic accusation, and eventual celebration, rediscovers his alter ego, Lycidas, as "Genius of the shoar" and at the same time as one with "all the Saints above" (lines 176ff.). The elegist-swain, too, is himself saved, perhaps by grace, from the territorial defensiveness associated with burial rites and grave monuments. He will go to "fresh woods and pastures new" tomorrow, unlike the survivors of Samson in Milton's biblical tragedy who will attend the hero's monument on feast days, inspired and yet enclosed by a figure of the old law.

These great poems rise above topical Independency, of course, and, to be sure, the headnote to *Lycidas* indicating a prophecy against "corrupted Clergy," added in the 1645 edition of Milton's *Poems*, could be taken generally rather than specifically. Nonetheless, by 1645 Milton was sufficiently disaffected by the established Anglican Church to have published *Of Reformation* and *Of Prelatical Episcopacy* (both in 1641), *The Reason of Church Government* (1642), in which he recalls how he felt "Church-outed" by the prospect of a ministerial career in the established church (Yale Prose, 1:823), *The Doctrine and Discipline of Divorce* (1643), and *Areopagitica*

(1644), as well as other radically Puritan polemics. Because the divorce tracts and *Areopagitica* question Presbyterian and prelatical authority, biographers accordingly place Milton in the Independent camp by 1644. There may be some lesser topicality in other religious poems in the 1645 *Poems*—"On the Morning of Christ's Nativity," for example, can be related to the church calendar, and the miniature Latin epic, "In Quintum Novembris," on the Gunpowder plot (written when Milton was seventeen) implicitly celebrates a Protestant holiday. Unlike *Lycidas*, however, these poems do not confront clerical authority in the Church of England. Perhaps a stronger case can be made for the longest work in the 1645 *Poems*, "A Masque presented at Ludlow Castle, 1634" (Comus) as in some ways a Puritan theatrical piece with ecclesiological overtones. Maryann McGuire, for instance, has argued that it conveys Puritan objections to the loose morals of the royal court, to games on the Sabbath, and to the sullied body of the Laudian church establishment.[17]

The unsullied lady is of course a traditional figure of *Ecclesia*, a figure perhaps also suggested in Milton's sonnet of 1643, "Ladie, that in the prime of earliest youth / Wisely hath shun'd the broad way and the green." She is "Virgin wise and pure" in an allusion to Matt. 25:1–13, the parable of the bridegroom who rewards the wise virgin's care and her "deeds of light" (lines 9–10). On this level of meaning, the sonnet may invite comparison with Donne's Holy Sonnet, "Show me deare Christ, thy spouse, so bright and cleare" (ca. 1615), in which the same allusion is transparently ecclesiological. Donne's poem may remind us in its startling paradox of the keen emotions felt by both the churched and the church-outed over the important issue of the visible church:

> Dwells she with us, or like adventuring knights
> First travaile we to seeke and then make love?
> Betray kind husband thy spouse to our sights,
> And let myne amorous soule court thy mild Dove,
> Who is most trew, and pleasing to thee, then
> When she is embrac'd and open to most men.[18]

Milton's "ladie" conceit may not be topical at all. However, he did address the problem of opposition to his Independent views on matters of church discipline in several explicitly topical sonnets. "On the Detraction which followed upon my Writing Certain Treatises" (1645 or 1646) is a plea for a careful reading of his divorce tracts by both his opponents and his champions, by whoever "bawl for freedom in thir senseless mood, / And still revolt when Truth would set them free" (lines 9–10). Milton may have had in mind anecdotes such as one given by his detractor, Thomas Edwards, in *Gangraena* (1646):

> There are two Gentlemen of the Inns of Court, civil and well dis-
> posed men, who out of novelty went to hear the women preach, and after
> Mistris *Attaway* the Lace-woman had finished her exercise, these two
> Gentlemen had some discourse with her, and among other passages she
> spake to them of Master *Milton's* Doctrine of Divorce, and asked them
> what they thought of it, saying, it was a point to be considered of; and that
> she for her part would look more into it, for she had an unsanctified hus-
> band, that did not walk in the way of *Sion*, nor speak the language of
> *Canaan*; and how accordingly she hath practised it in running away with
> another womans Husband.[19]

"Divorcers" seem to have been regarded as Independents by other detractors such as Baillie and Clement Walker. Baillie does concede, "I doe
not know certainly whither this man [Milton] professeth *Independency* (albeit all the Hereticks here whereof ever I heard, avow themselves Independents)." Walker has no such left-handed compunction in affiliating this
"Libertine that thinketh his Wife a Manacle . . . after the Independent fash-
ion" with instigators of war against the king—the Independents intending
"to pull down Monarchy, and set up Anarchy."[20] Milton's reputation as an
Independent and Divorcer apparently preceded his fame as a poet for the
remainder of his life.

The "tailed" sonnet of twenty lines, "On the New Forcers of Conscience
under the Long Parliament" (1646), attempts to normalize the Independent
position on church governance in contrast to Presbyterian reactionaries like
Baillie (the "Scotch what d'ye call" of line 12) in the Westminster Assembly of Divines, where "New Presbyter is but old Preist writt large" (line
20). For Milton, Congregational ideals as well as his views on marriage
and divorce were threatened by the "classic Hierarchy" (line 7) of the Presbyterian "classis," and by the dictates of the assembly prescribing the *Directory of Public Worship* as a replacement for the *Book of Common Prayer*.
The new authority lent itself to the old clerical abuse of plurality—"the
widow'd whore Plurality" (line 3)—and impeded the spontaneous form of
worship favored by Independents rejecting the prayer book. The obscuran-
tist attitude of Presbyterians and of the public at large that impedes liberal-

izing church governance and divorce laws is also criticized in Milton's sonnet of the same year, "A book was writt of late call'd *Tetrachordon*."

More affirmatively, the Westminster Assembly and Parliament may have influenced Milton's translations of Psalms 80–88 in 1648.[21] Because of their potential liturgical significance, translated psalteries could reflect ecclesiastical controversy, and the assembly and the House of Commons supported more "common measure" translations outside of the King James Bible Psalms framed by the establishmentarian *Book of Common Prayer.* Milton's version is close to common measure in prosody and, as William B. Hunter has pointed out, coincides with a group of Psalms assigned for revised translation by the assembly.[22] Common measure, of course, is also a folk meter and lends itself to popular melodies any congregation could sing. It therefore encourages congregational participation in the liturgy or a popular ownership of forms of worship. "Dost thou shew wonders among the dead: or shall the dead rise up again, and praise thee" (Ps. 88:10 in the *Book of Common Prayer,* the same as the King James translation) is recast in Milton's version as,

> Wilt thou do wonders on the dead,
> Shall the deceas'd arise
> And praise thee *from their loathsom bed*
> *With pale and hollow eyes?*

From Milton's headnote, these "are the very words of the Text, translated from the original" with additions clearly marked by italics. Milton intends to follow the Hebrew and to respect the sanctity of the Psalm's literal meaning. Perhaps in a small way he also asserts the poet's own authority in a congregational exercise of witnessing God's word.

A degree of aesthetic individualism also asserts itself in the eight Psalms Milton translated five years later, in 1653, apparently in a two-week period. Not in common meter, these translations are sophisticated and varied in prosody, often containing run-on lines, the rhythm of the epics to come. They are not a congregational psaltery, yet they seem a kind of testimony, their contexts perhaps carrying Milton's burdens as well as confirming his metrical talents. Mary Powell, his first wife, had died in the previous year, and, as his blindness became total, he was also beset with ad hominem attacks on his defense of the Commonwealth government. In the King James version, Ps. 6:7 reads, "My beauty is gone for very trouble: and worn away because of all mine enemies." In Milton's translation, the image seems more hauntingly personal: "mine Eie / Through grief consumes, is waxen old and dark / I'th midst of all mine enemies that mark." To modern readers, this anticipates *Samson Agonistes*, where a blind hero seeks his own way out of singular darkness.

In more obvious ways, Milton's official position with the Commonwealth government influenced his sonnet on Cromwell (1652) and the still-famous sonnet expressing grief and outrage at the massacre of Piemontese Protestants (1653). The Cromwell sonnet was occasioned by the attempts of certain members of the Independent clergy to set up an established church, one that would have limited tolerance for dissenters. Presumably these Independents did not know "what to make of their victory" over the king. For Milton, the "hireling wolves" of a state-funded church (line 14), perhaps any stipendiary clergy, and the continuing practice of tithing are the peacetime foes of true Independency and ought to be overthrown by the lord protector:

> . . . peace hath her victories
> No less renown'd than warr, new foes arise
> Threatning to bind our souls with secular chains:
> Help us to save free Conscience from the paw
> Of hireling wolves whose Gospell is their maw.
>
> (lines 10–14)

In the sonnet to Henry Vane the Younger (1652), also an Independent in the public eye and a member of the government, Milton again praises a leader of the republic for his mature wisdom in managing "Both spirituall power and civill" (line 9). These topical sonnets demonstrate Milton's republican and civic idealism, but they also witness Christian liberty in a civil life enhanced by a rightly informed Independency. Milton is speaking as a patriot and, too, as a member of an essential congregation linking true believers to each other and to Christ. This same attitude underlies and enhances the struggles of soul and mind in his greater poetry as well.

1

Hurled Bones and
the Noble Mind

Commentary on *Lycidas* is now a long procession, and finding the right place in line for what follows may first require noticing some near positions. In his discussion of *Lycidas*, Jon Lawry emphasizes that the poem's agon is caused by "the apparent distance between the stance of earth and Heaven," a distance resolved by the transcending power of "eager thought" in the speaker's mind, one able to retain "incomplete propositions" even as it moves conclusively toward a sense of heavenly union.[1] In the course of this struggle, pastoral imagery of the classical kind and its "Olympian stance" appear "less potent and therefore less real than the oceanic tempests of loss," although, ironically, these same pastoral images hint at renovation, faith, and immortality.[2] This very "impotence" provokes the speaker's eventually right judgment, that of Jove's heavenly perspective. From this perspective, nature and man can be reconciled as well, since death, in the doctrine underlying the poem, derives from original sin and not from nature itself. The forces of nature do not kill Lycidas, but rather the "contrivance" of the faithless bark, implicitly linked to Satan and to sin.[3] By the end of the poem, consolation, salvation, and celebration have united the two stances. The poem's shepherds are not only comforted but also related to heaven along with Lycidas, signifying the renovation of society through the agency of Christ. For the speaker, too, "the isolation of death is revoked." Hence, even though *Lycidas* is metaphorical, it is also doctrinal.[4]

Lawrence Hyman, on the other hand, argues that restoration in *Lycidas* is not a doctrinal effect, and that, in our response to the poem, doctrine and aesthetics remain opposed: "It is the pastoral tradition, particularly as this tradition is given renewed power by Milton's deliberate and highly conscious control over his form, not our twentieth-century skepticism, that makes us see the resurrection in *Lycidas* as an aesthetic experience rather than as a religious belief."[5] The "feelings within the poem and the feelings that exist outside of the poem" are distinct. The allusion to Christian resurrection in the poem "is simply another metaphor" for a general, imagined sense of renovation: "It is not poetry that is brought into the higher syntheses of Christianity, but rather the Christian *consolatio* that is brought into the imaginative experience of the poem."[6]

Perhaps somewhere between reading *Lycidas* as a celebration of aestheticism and as a celebration of doctrine are a number of analyses of the speaker's identity, his maturing sense of self as both poet and priest. Stanley Fish, for example, believes that "the suppressing of the personal voice is the poem's achievement" and that, eventually, "the determined anonymity of *Lycidas* should remind us that the poet's fierce egoism is but one half of his story."[7] Peter M. Sacks relates the theme of loss to the elegist's maturing ego in more specifically Freudian terms: "The work of mourning involves a castrative moment of submission to death and to a necessary deflection of desire." Milton's text moves from an emphasis on mother and female figures to images of authoritative fathers, implying the speaker's discovery of "a trope for procreative force that outlasts individual mortality." The "crux in the mourning" is the allusion to Orpheus's death and to his mother's failure to protect him, "a recapitulated loss of the mother together with a scenario of castration." Here, the youth's immature "economy of sacrifice and reward" collapses, and "the notion of reward must be revised, a revision somehow earned more fully" by the submission to death on the part of the poet. Consolation is therefore found by the poet in "a resurgent yet displaced and spiritualized sexual energy" that will "triumph" over the images of castration in the text.[8]

To be sure, parts of the criticism are mutually exclusive. Nonetheless, a synthesis of doctrine, aesthetic effect, and psychological affect is possible in interpreting the poem, I believe, when we attend to the resonance of its recurrent symbol, the body of Lycidas. As the criticism repeatedly implies, Lycidas is a metaphorical and aesthetic figure of some kind and, of course, a saintly identity in the mind of the elegist. I would like to discuss not only the elegist's developing attitudes toward the metaphor as signifying his maturing identity but also his implicit concern for the right relationship between this identity and the ecclesiastical body experiencing the crisis of reformation. I hope to explain both the affectively reforming and Reformation psychology of Milton's pastoral voice by considering the

Pauline concept of the mystical body of the church as an important antecedent of *Lycidas*, one linking the crisis of mind and personality to that of
ecclesiastical discipline and doctrine in ways that illuminate the meaning
of the poem.[9]

We might first consider that the headnote added to *Lycidas* in the 1645
edition of Milton's *Poems* is itself a developmental kind of statement, one
suggesting the maturing identity of a congregational poet—i.e., a pastoral
elegist who will demonstrate both personal and ecclesiastical reformation:
*"In this Monody the Author bewails a learned Freind, unfortunatly drown'd
in his passage from Chester on the Irish Seas, 1637. And by occasion foretells the ruin of our corrupted Clergy then in their height."* Monody is of
course a song by one voice, and the term connotes the solitariness and
introspection of the singer perhaps more than would eclogue or elegy. The
second sentence, however, if indignant in tone, is more spiritually nurturing and congregational in its underlying attitude and significance. The image of the drowned friend will be balanced, perhaps outweighed, by that of
corruption in the visible church, a prophecy embracing "our" clergy. This
harsh but productive witnessing is in turn comparable to a communal ministry and its exhortative liturgy.[10]

Elements of a lyric psychology of ruin leading to reform in the poetic
text derive from the author's historical sense of the church discipline of
threatened and actual excommunication in the course of pastoral nurture.
In the historical context regarded by Milton as helping to explain the structure of the poem, pastoral discipline and nurture have been wrongly and
selfishly practiced by the established hierarchy of pastors and prelates. One
implied promise of the poem, however, is that church discipline can be
rightly understood and practiced by a congregation purged of hierarchic
influence, and by the individual Christian accepting his mature identity as
minister, or shepherd, by virtue of his membership in the mystical body of
the church. In the poetic text, the pilot's foretelling of ruin and his witness
against "corrupted," morally dead clergy can also be understood as a psychologically displaced prophecy against the swain's own self-protecting,
immature aestheticism, his hierarchic stage of artistic development dem-
onstrating a "noble" (*Lycidas,* line 71) but also infirm elegiac practice and
persona. Hence, the polemical ramifications of the "occasion" afforded by
personal grief are continuous with the lyric's expressive celebration of a
maturing, congregational personality, the mind of a rightly shepherding poet.

The monodistic voice in the text first would preserve the ego's precedence
and supposed authority. Its self-centered aestheticism, work associated with

some future inscription, and the elegist's own "destin'd urn" (line 20), mounts a defense against an authentic obligation—one implied by the omniscient and prophetic tone of the headnote—to apply personal grief ecclesiastically and beyond the self. The monodist's bewailing "a learned" friend, unlike the eventual application of learning and grief, begins as a centripetal kind of mythography, an "Inwraught" (line 105) exercise by a fearful and perhaps somewhat tyrannical ego, to borrow the term from its later context describing Camus's aesthetic vestments ("Inwraught with figures dim"). The "uncouth swain" (line 186), however, a term implying a less egoistic yet more mature identity for the elegist, will denigrate or abandon the aesthetic, cultic structures such as the "fondly" dreamt wish for mythic significance and protection (line 56), or the evoked appearance of a flower-strewn body, the work of a "Sicilian muse" (line 133). These have displaced an ego threatened by the consequence of sin and by the actual, "dred voice" of reform (line 132). The pilot's "dred voice" is also a consequence of sin and therefore in keeping with the harsh reality of death. However, unlike the monodist's previous, mythographic image of "the blind *Fury*" (line 75), that of the pilot's voice and threatening presence nearly reforms the procession of mourners and is a more useful and rightly reasoned liturgy, one reifying the transcendent integrity of the mystical body of the church even as it castigates the selfishness of established clerics, figured as merely appetitive bodies.

In his monodistic state of mind, mythographic (rather than piloting) pastoralism is a tempting, purgatorial kind of contract, a covenant of works between the elegist and his sources, "Sisters of the sacred well" (line 15). This covenant derives from a youthful ego's supposed dominion over death as well as life. It is a structuring reaction to the threat of losing control over the efficacy of works—here, textual or poetic works circumscribing death and expressing ambition. The pilot's speech implicitly demeans this covenant and the cultic, prescribed tradition of aesthetic limits with which the monodistic ego has become invested. In the more fully authorized context introduced by the pilot's speech, aesthetic works are better related to deeds as expressions of mature faith, a faith admitting the sinful causes of mortality and acknowledging that salvation is ultimately unaffected by works in themselves. The supposed authority of expressive lyricism in the opening lines of the poem will be subsumed by prophetic lyricism, because mythographic pastoralism, like the mistaken discipline and disciplining of the traditional clergy, is too often work without faith, the mere extension of an ego protecting itself. Piloting pastoralism, on the other hand, lyrically expresses faith even as it promises true discipline by means of deeds. Eventually, another authorial, or omniscient and authorized, voice will declare that the "uncouth swain" sang expressively—"Thus sang . . . to th'oaks and rills" (line 186)—yet the swain who is now identified as such and authoritatively fixed in the pastoral setting is also imagined entering future, uncircumscribed contexts: "To morrow to fresh woods, and pastures new" (line 193). His expressiveness here seems to transcend both a monodistic self obsessed with egoistic grief and the authorial self drawn to a historical crisis, although both aspects of the elegist's personality can serve the mystical body. The last line of the poem, accordingly, is expressively figurative and historically prophetic. The ending implies that a new authorial voice is quoting or somehow paraphrasing the swain, a lyric laborer; yet this last expressive effect, ambiguously assigned to swain or narrator, may also seem to generate a voice that is simultaneously subjective and objective, one singing in the mystical body of the church rather than in the confines of prescriptive pastoralism.

"My destin'd urn" had been a safe but sad boundary for the elegist's identity, and its terminal imagery is metonymous with supposedly safe pastoral vehicles ensuring self-preservation.[11] In the end, however, this artifact is like that vehicle conveying the elegist's alter ego, Lycidas—the "perfidious bark" (line 100), a work failing to sustain him. The monodist's fear of dissolution, however, is contravened by the pilot's authorized predictions of the kind of dissolution that necessarily precedes reform. This voice, also part of the swain's labor but one not limited by the "Bitter constraint" (line 6) of subjective grieving, breaks down the ego's artifacts and its protective boundaries in the course of its authorized and more productive ministry of witness. Without a reforming kind of dissolution or its prospect, Lycidas might have developed that "Inwraught" identity of his mentors— "old Damoetas" (line 36) and the "reverend Sire" (line 103), Camus, the antecedents of an established, unproductive clergy. Instead, he is claimed by the pilot as a "young swain" anticipating future reformation, and he exists in the pilot's mind as a paradigm for what ought to be the reformed church ("How well could I have spar'd for thee young swain, / A now of such as for their bellies sake" (lines 113–14)). The pilot displays the keys of more fruitful instruction and liturgy than Camus can provide. His keys instruct sinners, opening their minds to the importance of forgiveness. Although it is "dred," his voice significantly reforms the pastoral liturgy of grief; it incorporates the reality of mortal dissolution with the mystical body of the church as a whole, the essential church that exists simultaneously in heaven, in the congregation, and in the mind.

The fresh woods and pastures of the swain's own genius may attend to the "dred" voice of authorized, reformed pastoralism again, and here we might compare the mature, pastoral voice of Milton's later sonnet, "On the Late Massacher in Piemont" (1655):

> Avenge O Lord, thy slaughter'd Saints, whose bones
>   Lie scatter'd on the *Alpine* mountains cold,
>   Ev'n them who kept thy truth so pure of old
>   When all our Fathers worship't Stocks and Stones,
> Forget not: in thy book record their groans
>   Who were thy Sheep and in their antient fold
>   Slain by the bloody *Piemontese* that roll'd
>   Mother with Infant down the Rocks. Their moans
> The Vales redoubl'd to the Hills, and they
> To Heav'n. Their martyr'd blood and ashes sow
> O're all th' *Italian* fields where still doth sway
> The triple Tyrant: that from these may grow
>   A hunderd-fold, who having learnt thy way
>   Early may fly the *Babylonian* wo.

In this context, "thy book" (line 5) is not merely a funereal inscription invalidating anger and indignation. Rather, by recording affective sounds ("groans") and not dicta or names and statements, the Lord's text generates reformation transcendentally. Spatial boundaries seem to collapse when the sounds of suffering are heard simultaneously by vales, hills, and heaven. Eventually, the image of mortal dissolution, the "scatter'd" bones (line 2) of these true Christians, may engender a Christian liberty of consciousness as well as of national circumstance. Instruction in "thy way / Early" motivates escape from "*Babylonian* wo" (lines 13–14), the depressing cultural limitation and psychology caused by seemingly secure but actually uninspired worship of "Stocks and Stones" (line 4), iconic structures established superstitiously or perfidiously.

The image of Lycidas's hurled bones also engenders an eventually liberated, ministerial consciousness. In a sense, like the bones, Lycidas has fled early from the "pledge" asserted by debilitated authority and its aesthetic "edge" or limit (*Lycidas*, lines 103–7), but the uncertain location of the bones encourages a better kind of liturgy than that of the "laureat herse" (line 151). The escape or direction of the elegist as well as his alter ego is toward the heavenly kingdom of "unexpressive nuptiall song" (line 176), an aesthetic liturgy beyond the margins of prescribed texts and egoistic structures. The hurled bones rest in a dynamic kind of peace, one comparable to the sanctified ubiquity of the mystical body and its expressive, unbound liturgy.

Exclusion as an edifying threat, the discipline symbolized by the pilot's keys and by the "two-handed engine" (130), is of course part of the literature of the ongoing Reformation encouraged by Milton. The lyric process of grieving in the poem and the reformation of "bodies" in various cultic and institutional senses are comparable to Milton's antiprelatical exhortations to reform the Christian community through improved understandings and applications of church discipline in clerical administration as well as in liturgics. In *Of Reformation*, "pure Religion" necessarily requires

> to cashier, and cut away from the publick body the noysom, and diseased tumor of Prelacie, and come from Schisme to *unity* with our neighbour Reformed sister Churches, which with the blessing of *peace* and *pure doctrine* have now long time flourish'd; and doubtles with all hearty *joy*, and *gratulation*, will meet, and welcome our Christian *union* with them, as they have bin all this while griev'd at our strangenes and little better than separation from them. (Yale Prose, 1:598)

One justification for so dismembering the ministerial hierarchy in order to reform it is that the bishops themselves have misunderstood or misapplied the discipline of excommunication, using it "peremptorily" and as a "peece of pure Primitive Divinity." "This most mild, though withall dredfull, and inviolable Prerogative of Christs diadem excommunication servs for nothing with them, but to prog, and pandar for fees, or to display their pride." Valid excommunication, on the other hand, does not seek "to bereave or destroy the body." If properly applied, "it seekes to save the Soule by humbling the body," and "by Fatherly admonishment, and Christian rebuke, to cast it into godly sorrow, whose end is joy, and ingenuous bashfulnesse to sin." Excommunication is therefore not a seemingly commercial act but rather a form of Christian education: If the "godly sorrow, whose end is joy, and ingenuous bashfulnesse to sin . . . can not be wrought, then as a tender Mother takes her Child and holds it over the pit with scarring words, that it may learne to feare, where danger is, so doth excommunication as deerly, and as freely without money, use her wholsome and saving terrors" (Yale Prose, 1:608).

In the *Institutes*, Calvin discusses this teaching authority and ministry by first citing Eph. 4:10–13: In the work of ministry, Christ assigned some as apostles, others as prophets, evangelists, pastors, and teachers, "for the building up of the body of Christ, until we all reach the unity of the faith and of the knowledge of the Son of God, to perfect manhood, to the measure of the fully mature age of Christ." Those rejecting the spiritual food of these nurturing offices, in Calvin's view, "deserve to perish in famine and hunger." He continues, "The face of God shines upon us in teaching"; one sought the face of God in the temple sanctuary because there "the teaching of the law and the exhortations of the prophets were a living image of God, just as Paul asserts that in his preaching the glory of God shines in the face of Christ [2 Cor. 4:6]."[12] The authority of the keys conferred on the apostles to forgive sins is a similarly hortatory, educative office, a duty to preach and counsel reconciliation to God through Christ: "Therefore, in the communion of saints, our sins are continually forgiven us by the ministry of the church itself when the presbyters or bishops to whom this office has been committed strengthen godly consciences by the gospel promises in the hope of pardon and forgiveness. This they do publicly and privately as need requires."[13] In a rightly reformed church, "the keys have an indissoluble bond with the Word." Paradoxically, however, the Word is preached "through men like us." We can therefore "best evidence our piety and obedience toward God if we show ourselves teachable toward his minister, although he excels us in nothing." God hid wisdom "in weak and earthen vessels in order to prove more surely how much we should esteem it." Moreover, "this human ministry which God uses to govern the church is the chief sinew by which believers are held together in one body."[14]

Milton refers to the keys of disciplinary authority in *The Reason of Church Government*, where he attacks the secular reliance of bishops in enforcing the ministry of censure:

> Surely much rather might the heavenly ministry of the Evangel bind her self about with farre more pearcing beams of Majesty and aw by wanting the beggarly help of halings and amercements in the use of her powerful Keies. For when the Church without temporal support is able to doe her great works upon the unforc't obedience of men, it argues a divinity about

her. But when she thinks to credit and better her spirituall efficacy, and to win herself respect and dread by strutting in the fals visard of worldly autority, tis evident that God is not there; but that her apostolick vertu is departed from her, and hath left her *Key-cold*. (Yale Prose, 1:832–33)

Self-esteem and the fear of shame should be motives enough for godly behavior, attitudes instilled by the laity as well as by ministers in part from the threat of holy discipline by the congregation as a whole.[15] This manner of closing the door is instructional and therapeutic for the sinner, a "vehement cleansing medicin" that is also "a mortifying to life, a kind of saving by undoing. . . . as the mercies of wicked men are cruelties, so the cruelties of the Church are mercies" (Yale Prose, 1:847).

In *Lycidas*, the pilot's foretelling of ruin for a corrupt clergy is also nurturing. It is within the mood of instructed repentance informing the mortal, and therefore sinful, elegist, bringing him closer to the author's position of relating grief to prophetic witness. The pilot's voice asserts the continuity between pastoral mourning and pastoral discipline. His is also the discriminating office of the mature minister and preacher, the overseer who guides sternly, the pilot with "mitr'd locks" who "stern bespake" (*Lycidas,* line 112). His guidance and the ministerial leadership of the entire church body urge the sinner to overcome his alienation through their disciplinary projections. Such is the right use of the keys of authorized forgiveness by means of instruction from those who do know how to handle a sheep hook. Whatever its specific tenor, the "two-handed engine at the dore" that "Stands ready to smite once and smite no more" (lines 130–31) is generally the application of mortifying discipline through exhortation and image. Like the rhetorical "engines of terror" Milton recommends for preachers searching the hearts of sinners (Yale Prose, 1:846), it mainly "Stands ready," its force exercised in forbidding prospect, it is hoped, rather than in actual use by the communion of saints.

The mature, authorized aesthetic that develops by means of the ritualistic processes of mourning giving way to affective, prophetic assertions of educative love and faith invests the pastoral artist with a more productive consciousness of his own membership in the communion of saints: "At last he rose, and twitcht his mantle blew: / To morrow to fresh woods, and pastures new" (*Lycidas,* lines 192–93). Putting on his mantle against the night concedes the elegist's heritage of sin and mortality, but his earthbound existence in time is also the occasion for his incorporating with "him that walkt the waves" (line 173). The Christian paradox of death as consummation and consequent engendering of timeless life within the mystical body influences the elegist's projection of his alter ego, Lycidas, in heaven, entertained by "all the Saints" singing "In solemn troops, and sweet societies" (lines 178–79), the dead singer and builder of lofty rhymes (line 11) now hearing a song that is "unexpressive" and "nuptiall" (line 176). The image of the alter ego who is also "Genius" and "good / To all that wander" (lines 184–85) conveys a similarly mystical incorporation, one also necessitated by mortal peril and the errors of fallen, wandering humanity. Paradoxically, the "unexpressive" song is framed within the describable song, a "*Dorick* lay," yet seems to transcend the frame as well in a way that is analogous to the reforming of the elegist's understanding of mortality and of the function of pastoral aesthetic. The elegist is therefore objectified in the third person, finally, to indicate the self's nearing the completion of identity, even if the terms of maturity, "the uncouth swain" (line 186), are humble and limited in tone. The swain sings in time, history, and convention, first discovering that his self-conscious exercise in mourning commemorates the self-absorption, the alienation, of the artist displacing the crisis of sin with the crisis of technique, then later discovering that his capacity for faith and love is greater than the sum of these parts. The dread voice is loving, declaring the integrity of the communion of saints on earth as it relates death to an ecclesiastical significance taking shape in the swain's song. All these voices, however seemingly disparate, are counterpointed parts of the elegist's identity as a mortal sinner who will nonetheless experience sanctification and its eventual peace of conscience. The shift to omniscience at the close authorizes this complex yet "uncouth" identity.

The dread, witnessing voice is also the earthly counterpart of the loving choir of saints in heaven. It cooperates with the peace of conscience and ecclesiastical integrity experienced by the sanctified, individually and as members of the church. The "dred voice" and the "unexpressive" song are paradoxically the rightly harmonized vocal framework and sounds for accommodating not only the corrupt and the saved but also the variously insecure moods of the elegist. They imply a truly harmonious and firm identity of the whole human being, a mature structure of mind in which the dissolving, juvenile self is not just an alarming prospect but one that can be rightly celebrated. In this reformed context, work is not futile aestheticism but rather more like "works" in the theological sense, an act of worship. By the end of the poem, a context of reformed worship has been constructed and expressed, one supplanting the unreliable context of worship—the unloving, exclusionary rite or merely negative utterance, forms like the "perfidious bark / Built in th'eclipse, and rigg'd with curses dark, / That sunk so low that sacred head of thine" (lines 100–102).

Perfidy, of course, is the foreseeable outcome of superstition and the misapplied pronouncements of hierarchy. It can result from the dicta or works of "Blind mouths!" in the pilot's speech (line 118), the works of those excluding out of narrow selfishness rather than out of love, not having "learn't ought els the least / That to the faithfull herdmans art belongs!" (lines 120–21), and producing, "when they list, their lean and flashy songs" (line 123). The exclusionary pastorate of privilege and sinecure, unlike the reformed pastorate of loving discipline and faith, cannot manage a worthwhile liturgy, one that is a work of the people. Instead, such pastors "scramble" at the congregational "feast" and "shove away the worthy bidden guest" (lines 116–17). What may seem song at first is really a perfidious kind of discipline in their case, a liturgical aesthetic merely "flashy" or, again, one actually "rigg'd with curses dark," to cite the associated context.

Unreformed liturgy not only works to protect a sinfully greedy ego and its boundaries, but is also relatable to the elegist's mood of "Bitter constraint," his sense of unhappy duty compelling him to "pluck" and "Shatter" laurel, myrtle, and ivy out of season (lines 1–7). His bitterness at beginning the labor of lyric grieving complicates mere convention by introducing the youthfulness of the elegist as well as Lycidas, and by implying an at least vague sense of longing for a more mature kind of aesthetic. The mature aesthetic, we can gather later, would not be prompted strictly by occasion but by a ripening inspiration, an edifying muse that would develop the speaker as well as his text into states more closely approximating "the unexpressive nuptiall song" of a sanctified community of singers. The mood of constraint, however, first leads him toward delineated works, with the inscribed urn as partial compensation, he imagines, for his monody. This aesthetic covenant of works is apparently justified by the elegist's prospect of the unpreserved, unsung body exposed to an unshaped nature, to the water and wind, without "som melodious tear" as "meed" or due reward for inspired labor (line 14). Lycidas "knew / Himself to sing, and build the lofty rime," and therefore an obligation exists: "Who would not sing for *Lycidas*?" (lines 10–11). But, the conventional, dictated trope of immortality produced by aesthetic commemoration is ironically unsettling. The "fair peace" (line 22) the elegist would project as a compensation addressed by "some gentle muse" (line 19) in the mortal future is not a worshipful or sanctified context, and the image of aesthetic ("fair") calm is already compromised by the disappointing resonance of "With lucky words favor my destin'd urn" (line 20). Such tribute, perhaps one associated with superstitious pronouncements, would not involve the inscriber as pastoral artist in the ministerial sense developing in the poem's later contexts, nor would it consider the dead builder of rhymes to be a nurturing genius and guide, a ubiquitous presence whose new works are sufficiently expressive of glory. The pretended involvement of this first alter ego, the urn inscriber and favorer, is more a power display than a communion. Having announced his possessive seduction of the sisters by admonishing them—"Hence with denial vain, and coy excuse" (line 18)—the elegist imagines, or aesthetically begets, a favored urn in order to limit and therefore control the boundaries of his self-portrait. The "sad occasion," when so treated as one of covenanted works by the inscriber ego fulfilling the elegist's wish, anticipates the appetitive dicta of the "Blind mouthes" feeding selfish hierarchy. "Lucky" and "as he passes" (lines 20–21) imply the latent perfidiousness and future indifference of such unreformed, clerical singers as well.

The tribute to pastoral kinship in youth is similarly more contractual than creatively inspired, relatable by "For" to the "need" and "favour" of compensation, even if the setting is rationalized as nurturing places of labor: "For we were nurst upon the self-same hill, / Fed the same flock by fountain, shade, and rill" (lines 23–24). Here the grieving elegist would shape the past not only to establish mutuality but also to make memory conform to his craving for artifact uncomplicated by a creator's sinfulness, and for a world seemingly without the necessity of atonement. Sin is accordingly nearly excluded, and the foresight of losing innocence is subordinated to "our song" (line 36). The hints of disorder and mortality in "Rough Satyrs," and "Fauns with clov'n heel," and "old Damoetas," consequences of the heritage of sin, are factitiously contained, or nearly so, safely enshrined within the aestheticism of pastoral temporality and the margins of Cambridge allegory:

> Together both ere the high Lawns appear'd
> Under the opening eyelids of the morn,
> We drove afeild, and both together heard
> What time the grayfly winds her sultry horn,
> Batning our flocks with the fresh dews of night,
> Oft till the star that rose in Evning bright,
> Toward Heav'ns descent had sloapt his westring wheel.
> Mean while the rurall ditties were not mute,
> Temper'd to th' oaten flute;

Rough Satyrs danc't, and Fauns with clov'n heel,
From the glad sound would not be absent long,
And old *Damoetas* lov'd to hear our song.

(lines 25–36)

The scene, while moving peacefully and beautifully toward a tuneful night, repressively manages fear and desire by melodious effort—the satyrs dance; the fauns are charmed; aged authority is pleased. The tableau, however, does not reform or relate infirmity to atonement, but rather preserves it. Music here does not open the mind to the possibilities of "fresh woods" anticipated at the poem's second close of day, but instead accompanies the making of centripetal exercise, the song heard by three figures, its allegorical references having no real significance, as Samuel Johnson partially observed, because it has no "real passion," only aesthetic images supporting each other.[16] Loving "to hear" but without sufficient attention to sin is ultimately uncharitable, not nurturing. The young shepherds' attachment to Damoetas is established by pleasure in song, pleasure that is harmless enough but a love subordinating a better charity of aged authority—nurturing admonition. A past in which the consciousness of sin is repressed influences the present to be similarly redundant and unregenerating in its artistry. The "heavy change" noticed next because of Lycidas's absence (*Lycidas,* line 37) is also evaluated aesthetically, its significance subordinated to lyricism: "Such, *Lycidas*, thy loss to shepherds ear" (line 49). Even though the green landscape is gone (the "copses green / Shall now no more be seen, / Fanning their joyous leavs to thy soft layes" [lines 42–44]), nature still resembles or reciprocates the mood of the singer as monodist, not minister: "Thee Shepherd, thee the woods, and desert caves / With wilde Thyme, and the gadding vine o'regrown, / And all thir echoes mourn" (lines 39–41). While there is a certain order in this prescribed, mythographic effect in nature, the mourning echoes enclose or preserve grief and, correlatively, the alienated elegist and his mood of "heavy change." The burden of loss and the insecurity of actual nature, the Irish Sea or "the stormy *Hebrides*" (line 156), the world rightly witnessing mortality as the consequence of sin, are shut out by echo and repetition. Mutability may succumb to the artistic ego's intentional design, but its burden will not be delivered.

In this circumscribed context, one cultivated to ease or mask the necessity of witness and loving discipline, accusation is also redundant, expressing the monodist's alienation. The complaint against the nymphs, absent "when the remorseless deep / Clos'd o're the head of your lov'd *Lycidas*" (lines 50–51), again limits or contains the obligations of love by mythography rather than energizes them. The relegation to the nymphs of "love" as unsustaining affection serves to limit the significance of the word; although, as the mythographic context begins its inexorable elaboration, the monodist's self-denigration intensifies, finding its correlative in mythic geographies of resentment:

> Where were ye nymphs when the remorseless deep
> Clos'd o're the head of your lov'd *Lycidas*?
> For neither were ye playing on the steep,
> Where your old Bards, the famous Drüids lie,
> Nor on the shaggy top of *Mona* high,
> Nor yet where *Deva* spreds her wisard stream:
> Ay me, I fondly dream!
> Had ye bin there—for what could that have don?
> What could the Muse her self that *Orpheus* bore
> The Muse her self for her inchanting son
> Whom universal nature did lament,
> When by the rout that made the hideous roar
> His goary visage down the stream was sent,
> Down the swift *Hebrus* to the *Lesbian* shoar.

(lines 50–63)

In Milton's draft of the passage, the Muse had been described as looking ahead, beyond herself, and golden, implicitly generous:

> What could the golden-haired Calliope
> For her enchanting son
> When she beheld (the gods far-sighted be)
> His gory scalp roll down the Thracian lea.[17]

(lines 58–63)

The revision, however, returns us to "The Muse her self" as a contextual framing of Orpheus's birth, a redundancy that contains or confines the clause, "that *Orpheus* bore." Implicitly, the delivery or letting go through pain of prior identity is impeded by "her self," and the song of "her inchanting son" is drowned out by "the hideous roar" of envy. This singer's dismemberment is in turn contained spatially by "the swift *Hebrus*" and "the *Lesbian* shoar." His body's mythographically limited boundaries can then be contrasted, albeit again implicitly, with a more Reformation-minded geography of Spain, Scotland, home, and the stormy, wild ocean separating the tyrannical past yet occasioning a reformed future (lines 155–64).

Orpheus, of course, was also a doomed celebrant and pastoral minister. In the *Metamorphoses* to which Milton alludes, he is the son and priestly singer of Phoebus ("vatis Apollinei"),[18] and the protector and teacher of the proper rites of Bacchus ("orgia tradiderat" [*Meta.,* XI.93]), the god also grieving at the Maenads' savagery and the singer's loss (XI.68). Similar to Lycidas's scattered yet eventually harmonious presence, Orpheus is dismembered physically but fulfilled spiritually, consummately when his shade finds Eurydice a second, final time—"membra iacent diversa locis" [The poet's limbs lay scattered all around] (XI.50); "invenit Eurydicen cupidisque amplectitur ulnis; / hic modo coniunctis spatiantur passibus ambo" [{He} found Eurydice and caught her in his eager arms. Here now side by side they walk] (XI.63–64). The wondrous event ("mirum" [XI.51]) of the singing, severed head is also both dead and alive: 'flebile lingua / murmurat exanimis" [mournfully the lifeless tongue murmured] (XI.53). It evokes an echoing response from the river's banks: "respondent flebile ripae" [mournfully the banks replied] (XI.53). The grotesque fragmentation of the poet has not stopped his song, and his dripping head still receives the protection of Apollo (XI.56–60). Bacchus, here called Lyaeus (XI.67), "deliverer from care," in turn avenges his celebrant by transforming the Maenads into oaks, and then by deserting their fields for other vineyards, accompanied by a better group of devotees (XI.67–86). The Maenads had been angry at Orpheus for his indifference to them and his implicit contempt for their improper celebrations and appetites (XI.7). They accordingly extended their sacrilegious behavior into disrupting the hard work of field laborers, then into murder using the abandoned implements of tillage (XI.29–43). Unmoved by supplicating gesture as well as by his song, they demonstrated their impiety by killing the poet: "ad vatis fata recurrunt / tendentemque manus et in illo tempore primum / inrita dicentum nec quicquam voce moventem / sacrilegae perimunt" [They rushed back to slay the bard; and, as he stretched out his suppliant hands, uttering words then, but never before, unheeded, and moving them not a whit by his voice, the impious women struck him down] (XI.38–41).

Despite the important similarities with the fate of Lycidas, however, the narrative mode and the narrator's attitude in the contexts implied by the allusion are significantly different. Ovid's text, like the relationships it depicts, is inwrought, its changings promiscuously breeding myth after myth of various impieties and retributions, a text in perpetual motion reflecting the narrator's first inclination: "In nova fert animus mutatas dicere formas / corpora" [My mind is bent to tell of bodies changed into new forms] (I.1–2).

To be sure, there are moral possibilities in the narrative, but they are bound or impeded by the apparently endless, insatiable demands of mythographic appetite. The Orphic allusion in Milton's text, however, becomes a terminal case, its ornateness cracking under the onslaught of the elegist's questioning, and its moral significance, even if arrived at negatively, surviving as the mythography fades into the speaker's discontent. The questions simultaneously emphasize and undermine the elegist's mythographic tendency, the aestheticism protecting his ego. The dialogue with this aesthetic self is in turn undermined by the affective reaction, "Alas! What boots it with uncessant care," implying the alienation of a self caught up in bargaining. Disturbingly, the mythographic kind of context becomes increasingly untenable, yet also what the ego seems to crave most, the event continuous with fame, "the spur that the clear spirit doth raise / (That last infirmity of noble mind) / To scorn delights, and live laborious dayes" (*Lycidas,* lines 70–72). The covenant of works, here a kind of purgatorial aesthetic, displaces appetite with egoism; it does not develop a mature, moral psychology. Even if the aim is heavenly, a covenant so compromised is infirm, wrongly preserving the juvenile identity yet remaining in "noble mind."

Phoebus's reply to the prospect of the "*Fury* with th'abhorred shears" (line 75) cutting off the poet's life suggests an overcompensating ego, the ego here displaced as the Apollonian, protective father of the poet. The reply is a reversion to the authority of external, hierarchic dicta after his looking into the abyss—the panic at dissolution and annihilation prosodically emphasized by the line's severe, medial pause: "And slits the thin-spun life. But not the praise, / *Phoebus* repli'd, and touch't my trembling ears" (lines 76–77). The "praise," "perfet witness" of Jove (line 82), and his pronouncement on works ("each deed" [line 83]) further magnify the craving for authoritative verbal designs against the unpredictable, wild act of "the blind *Fury*" and against the "broad rumor" that "lies" in an equally dark abyss of language (line 80). A more comforting reply, we can assume, should include the covenant of faith and grace, even though this Jovian witness can serve as an expedient distraction.

A more principled kind of heavenly justification by faith rather than by works is of course the traditional, reformed view found in *De Doctrina.* Even though it does emphasize "the works of faith," this view distinguishes between the merely formulaic works of the old law (perhaps implicitly as well of the remnants of the old law in Anglican practice) and the works of "living faith."[19] In this reading of Rom. 3:28 and James 2:17, 2:20, 2:26,

"Faith has its own works, which may be different from the works of the law. We are justified, then, by faith, but a living faith, not a dead one, and the only living faith is a faith which acts" (Yale Prose, 6:490). The cultural ramifications of the Gospel's better covenant and more heartfelt textualism result in the heritage of Christian liberty written in the heart by the Holy Spirit. The new dispensation also affects the pastorate: "'The priesthood being changed, there is made of necessity a change also in the law. . . . There ariseth another priest, who is made not after the law of carnal commandment'" (Heb. 7:12, 7:15–16; Yale Prose, 6:521). Opposed are adherents of legalistic discipline in the church who retain vestiges of the old law, and "this law not only cannot justify, it disturbs believers and makes them waver. It even tempts God, if we try to fulfil it." The supposed utility of the law and its works in teaching us the doctrine of sin can also be misleading. The whole Mosaic law, therefore, is repealed (Yale Prose, 6:529–30, 534). Christian liberty, however, develops a mature rather than childlike identity for the believer who can now better serve God in love and truth. There is no need for "magisterial ordinances which compel believers to uniformity or deprive them of any part of their freedom" (Yale Prose, 6:537, 541).

In *Lycidas*, the "perfidious bark" is comparable to the institutional structures that ostensibly carry a pastor and Christian but that actually betray him, if paradoxically sending him toward salvation and the role of "Genius" in this instance. The full exercise of Christian liberty, then, is achieved by Lycidas within the church's mystical body and not in the visible institution. This Christian liberty and laboring manhood is also about to be approached by the "uncouth swain" contemplating the "fresh woods and pastures new" inviting tomorrow's works of faith. The disciplinary impediments relatable to an unreformed egoism and its contractual, mythographic defenses, the works of an infirm if noble mind, are similarly perfidious structures. Ironically, on this occasion, they carry the elegist toward disillusionment, his "false surmise" (*Lycidas,* line 153). The "Bitter constraint" of the sad occasion expresses a problematic mood of grief and artistry laboring defensively, not yet expressively. The pilot, however, dissonant and iconoclastic in his "dred voice," seems utterly free from the mythographic context, unresponsive to its processional characters, yet somehow relatable to them in time and space: "Last came, and last did goe, / The Pilot of the *Galilean* lake" (lines 108–9). Like the pilot's attitude, if unlike his tone, a reformed consciousness of ministry suggests that "eager thought" (line 189) rather than "Bitter constraint" should be prior to work, just as faith is prior to loving works. Like the pilot in time and timelessly, the reformed consciousness approaches the same pastures and woods as the unreformed. The swain's attitude of enfranchisement at the poem's close, however, is significantly different from his initial mood of alienation. Such is the lyric inheritance of the pilot's keys. Hence, the pastures are new and the woods fresh, cleansed, as the sinner is purified and saved from spiritual death in the better covenant now rightly conveyed.

Earlier, sin, work, and death were topics challenging the ego's supposed dominion over the reality of time, but they were relegated to an unenlightened sense of gratification, their theological significance repressed by the mind's last infirmity. The elegist's considering release from the "shepherds trade" and its seemingly closed, perhaps profitless, economy ("What boots it with incessant care / To tend the homely plighted shepherds trade" [lines 64–65]) was not the edifying, piloting complaint of the mature Christian. Escaping from a covenant of "laborious dayes" (line 72) when he thought to "strictly meditate the thankless muse" (line 66) anticipates Christian liberty, but here the desire for freedom is subordinated to a rhetorical justification of the compulsion for fame: "Were it not better don as others use, / To sport with *Amaryllis* in the shade, / Or with the tangles of *Neaera*'s hair? / Fame is the spur" (lines 67–70). Hence, the shift from fame as rumor to fame as Jovian reward merely reconstructs the covenant of works preserving the juvenile ego. Imagining the dissolved body as a static icon signifying reward and fame and not as ministering in the work of faith preserves a similarly embalmed egoism. "To strew the laureat herse where *Lycid* lies" (151) is aesthetic work expressing fear but ironically deadening the occasion for a ministry of faith.

Rejecting the iconographic body and fame as worthwhile objects of aesthetic labor, therefore, liberates the ego previously displaced by the imagined corpse. The affective lament "Ay me!" admits both hope and fear, echoing yet repudiating the mythographic "AI" decorating Camus's vestments, their "edge / Like to that sanguine flowr inscrib'd with woe" (lines 105–6), in his guise as celebrant of an outworn, contractual covenant: "Ah! who hath reft, quoth he, my dearest pledge?" (line 107). The affective utterance of the Christian elegist, however, opens his mind to the Gospel's authoritative, informal, and paradoxical definitions of fame. The lament expressing the unreformed mind's lack of authenticity or authority in the two preceding lines ("For so to interpose a little ease, / Let our frail thoughts daily with false surmise" [lines 152–53]) now occasions the elegist's mature ministry of witness. It is as though the elegist, fatigued and disillusioned by his contextual artistry of floral cataloging, hears and heeds the voice of the real, a grace not given to Camus, who remains wrapped up in the aesthetics of grief, infirmly, or at least slowly, searching for forensic rather than prophetic answers. For the reformed elegist, Lycidas is better regarded as unavailable for ritualistic and perhaps reductive pledges. He is "to our moist vows deni'd" and indefinitely present. "Under the whelming tide," he "Visit'st" or "Sleep'st" (lines 157–60) in the liberated imagination of the elegist and in the indefinitely located but nonetheless certain presence of the mystical body. Here, the alter ego suggests the elegist's ego as Christologically contingent rather than mythographically and liturgically masterful, and therefore free, enfranchised: "So *Lycidas* sunk low, but mounted high" (line 172) hears "the unexpressive nuptiall song" (line 176); he hears a consummate text without the boundaries of prescribed articulation and does so "Through the dear might of him that walkt the waves" (line 173).

The reforming of a covenant of works into a subordinate context implying the ascent of the covenant of grace, where works express faith worshipfully, resolves the elegist's grief. The presence of Lycidas in heaven is nonetheless sensuously aesthetic, and the ministry of angels to him is somehow corporal, affective and sanctified healing or nurture: "With nectar pure his oozy locks he laves, / And hears the unexpressive nuptiall song (lines 175–76); "all the Saints above" (line 178) "entertain him"; "In solemn troops, and sweet societies" they sing "And wipe the tears for ever from his eyes" (lines 177–81). The elegist then assigns Lycidas a task of physical, cognitive, and perhaps psychological ministry that is coterminous with the completion of identity: "Hence forth thou art the Genius of the shoar, / In thy large recompence, and shalt be good / To all that wander in that perilous flood" (lines 183–85). Both the work of the future and the baptismal naming of the developed personality in terms of Christian work rather than pastoral ease are expressive of faith and adoration. The saints "singing in their glory move" as they minister to Lycidas (line 180); Lycidas in "large recompence . . . shalt be good"; his ministry will be to pilot or guide the erroneous, a task that is simultaneously a reward, an atonement, and also glorification. This admirable labor, like the saints' singing, does not cause salvation or fame, but rather expresses a prior condition of transferred merit from "him that walkt the waves."

The elegist in turn is assigned a laborer's title—"the uncouth swain" (line 186)—by a second authorial or authorized voice, similarly omniscient. The unknown, unsophisticated servant has accomplished a day's work by means of "quills" and thought, and now we know who he is under the eye of eternity—a humble worker who exalts the sanctified and prophesies against the unreformed. That "He toucht the tender stops of various quills, / With eager thought warbling his *Dorick* lay" (lines 188–89) reveals his willingness to hazard various modes of lyric witnessing within a larger frame of harmony; his task was to shift from mode to mode (or "mood" in line 87), yet at the same time maintain the integrity of the whole song. The swain's work is both glorification and atonement by means of the expressed rather than the unexpressive song. On earth, his presence and labor will demonstrate both mortal necessity and immortal possibility. He too can sink in the course of his ministry, but he is still meant for the task.

The sometimes sweet, sometimes dread voice of an ultimately nurturing church, the ministry of the communion of saints, is the elegist's paradigmatic lyric, one eventually absorbing the mythographic voices disguising the ego's fear of dissolution. Johnson's famous complaint against the aesthetic pastoralism of Lycidas—that "where there is leisure for fiction there is little grief," merely confusing and unmoving poetry, "irreverent combinations" of pastoral identities—is correct in part.[20] The monodist's searching for significance in the mode of mythographic pastoral does necessitate, however, his mature self-accusation of disillusionment. This enlightened condition of mind regards the real as a divine love that addresses sin and its consequent mortality rather than relegating our heritage to hierarchic displacements of egoism. The youth's fear of death, the elegist reveals, is really a fear of the ego's loss of dominion, his identity previously continuous with a fame threatened with interruption by the "blind *Fury*," then reiterated mythographically as "so much fame in Heav'n." Such stylized, displaced fear of death is a kind of "fiction," an expression not of theologically based grief but one closer to vain anger at discovering the reality of a complex self needing to experience the authority of educated forgiveness. The "sad imbroidrie" (line 147) of mythographic pastoralism ironically preserves this anger and seems to validate an undeveloped ego. This is a certain identity, but one in which sorrow, unlike the saved Lycidas, is dead. The dread voice, however, the pilot authorized to cooperate with Christ and with the Spirit, reanimates sorrow as a promise for "eager thought." Such occasional grace transforms monody into a lyric work of the communion of saints singing in heaven and in the mature, laboring mind.

2

Love, Death, and the
Communion of Saints

Milton's Twenty-Third Sonnet, probably composed in 1658 after the death
of his second wife, Katherine Woodcock, still affects many general readers, and modern critics justly celebrate the poem's haunting imagery and
tonal complexity. Milton's artistry nonetheless aims at enhancing a spiritual and reformist statement, one in which a psychology of grief is tied to a
theology of sin and to the doctrine of the communion of saints:

> Mee thought I saw my late espoused saint
>> Brought to me like *Alcestis* from the grave
>> Whom *Joves* great son to her glad husband gave
>> Rescu'd from death by force though pale and faint.
> Mine as whom washt from spot of child-bed taint
>> Purification in th' old law did save,
>> And such, as yet once more I trust to have
>> Full sight of her in heav'n without restraint,
> Came vested all in white, pure as her mind:
>> Her face was vail'd, yet to my fancied sight
>> Love, sweetness, goodness in her person shin'd
> So clear, as in no face with more delight.
>> But O as to imbrace me she enclin'd,
>> I wak'd, she fled, and day brought back my night.

For its many modern interpreters, the sonnet is sincere or authentic not
so much because it expresses Milton's sense of true religion but because its
dream imagery is somehow validated by the dreamer's emotional ambiva-
lence. Elizabeth Hill, for instance, regards the sonnet as a complex of dream

processes and unconscious projections of Milton himself in a state of mourning, and she identifies several oneiric psychologies that allow for the "condensation" of the dreamer's mixed emotions into a single dream image. The single image of the saint, she believes, includes Milton's various feelings for his first and second wives, Mary Powell and Katherine Woodcock, rather than for one wife or the other. Moreover, his survivor's guilt, like that of Admetus in Euripides' *Alcestis*, is consistent with unrealistic idealizations of a dead wife by a husband. The image of the saint is finally a suffering mind's attempt to lessen the impact of guilt.[1]

Such an approach is surely valuable as far as it goes, but it gains rather than loses critical usefulness, I think, when drawing from reformist as well as mythic allusions. Simply clinical when studied in themselves, the dynamics of the sonnet's dream psychology can better illuminate Milton's intent when we simultaneously consider the doctrinal significance of its spousal and purification imagery. Here, an interpretation employing depth psychology might also take into account the tropological emphasis of Marilyn L. Williamson's interpretation (quoting John Chydenius) in which the marriage of the poem is also "'the marriage of the soul when after sin it returns to God and is united with him.'" She develops Leo Spitzer's thesis that the sonnet has "a rising motion" beginning in pagan salvation, followed by ritual salvation in the old law, and ending in Christian salvation, where the espoused saint is also the bride of Christ. The theme of marriage, however, is a "countermovement," a "falling movement" resulting from the contrast between Alcestis's "glad husband" (line 3) and the saint's sad, isolated husband.[2]

Dixon Fiske and Kurt Heinzelman have also discussed relevant theological and aesthetic ramifications of the allusions to purification in the sonnet. Fiske sees the speaker's spiritual development as the poem's theme. The reference to purification in the old law of Leviticus and its implicit allusion to the Christian rite of churching for women complement the Alcestis simile as impure types of the new law experienced by the saint, and toward which the speaker must progress. Fiske cites Calvin's commentary on the churching ritual as a reminder that birth conveys the mother's spiritual pollution of original sin to the child. Milton therefore alludes to the doctrine of original sin and its physical result of hazardous childbirth while he indicates the speaker's longing to be purified himself. The old law typology is ironic in this context; its rules and symbols demonstrate their own inadequacy as vehicles of salvation and therefore compel one to turn to the saving doctrine of the new law. The speaker eventually transcends his first perceptions of the saint and realizes "that the satisfaction of his love must really depend upon a change in his own state rather than in hers." The speaker's waking to night and her fleeing from his vision dramatize "the insufficiency of the dreamer himself"; he is "still facing the task of purification that she has already accomplished."[3]

Kurt Heinzelman relates to the aesthetics of similes in the text a similar assumption about the speaker's developing awareness of human inadequacy. Like Admetus in Euripides' *Alcestis*, the speaker is first drawn to the "'cold consolation'" of a fabricated image of his wife as she appeared before her death. The speaker cannot yet articulate "the greater life promised by God" within a "context of human loss." Courageously, however, he decides to live in the context of loss at the poem's conclusion, having been narcissistically tempted "to embrace his own graven image," the figurative presence of his wife generated by "the resemblance-making power of the poet." Since "he chooses to awake," he therefore "concedes the proper limits of the human will" on earth before an eventual reunion in heaven. Accordingly, "temporal restraints return" at the sonnet's close when day brings back "my night."[4] We may take such interpretations further, I think, and then find a somewhat different spiritual emphasis in the poem.

The husband's discovery of spiritual limits, then, his dramatized "insufficiency" and his projected image of the saint as an aspect of himself are primarily attitudes of displaced guilt. His first image is that of himself confronted by a reminder of death, love, and sanctification for which he is responsible, at least partly, by a possessive association: "my late espoused saint." The dream is therefore implicitly occasioned by the speaker's desire not for sanctification alone but for punishment and sanctification. Theologically, this is to participate fully in the new covenant as mortal sinner and immortal saint, and to sustain one's dialogue with God by means of the complaint of losing sanctification now as well as by anticipating it. Although the dream wish for freedom from guilt, time, and perhaps from a consciousness of mortality is conveyed by the image of the saint, this desire is accompanied by a censoring dream wish for the repeated but shallow security of daily grief and its clear, egoistic boundaries of self-denial.[5] Both wishes necessitate the concept of a mystical body to subsume them.

Prescribed, unreformed rites of purification alluded to by the speaker in his recounting of the dream suggest structural impediments to a full, transcendent membership in the communion of saints. In this context, both mythography and law as similes display a threatened ego's retreat into systematic consciousness. The speaker's reluctance to let go of the self is a barrier to his incorporation in the mystical body's limitless embrace. The Alcestis and Leviticus allusions signify the defensiveness of an as yet unreformed ego, its self-serving attachment to systems and liturgies having institutional authority. His comparing the saint to Alcestis and to one purified in the old law, and then his undermining of the likeness when he describes the saint herself, however, suggest he also regrets his initial attachment to system. He wants the embrace of redemptive, Christian love, but he is nonetheless a mortal sinner experiencing the anguish of guilt and looking initially for relief in ways that protect his ego. His sainted wife's initiating consummation (line 13), on the other hand, a compromise reversing sexual (or "sexist") authority, represents the speaker's deeper attachment to a psychology and theology of forgiveness, one less hierarchic, in the institutional sense, and more rightly reasoned in its prayerful working. This central and incomparable memory of the saint flees from a waking consciousness with which it is somehow at odds.

Here we might compare Adam's "evil Conscience" in *Paradise Lost* (X.849), when the potential of forgiveness for him is also clouded by egoism.[6] In the sonnet, as for a time in *Paradise Lost*, consciousness and conscience after the marital desire of sinners can rightly emphasize grief and guilt, but they can also preserve the ego's selfish boundaries and delay redemptive, rather than merely physical, consummation. In the sonnet, the visible world of day cooperates with the ego's wish for a punishing absence of consummate love, its desire for a definite boundary of night and day, a psychological limit that is also possessively "my night." When the ego confronts the sainted wife, an image of the speaker's actual incorporation with Christ as well as with her, it asserts its authority by restarting conventional time, but the "I" that "wak'd" keeps the speaker, like Adam, "in a troubl'd Sea of passion tost" (X.718).

Some of the traditional as well as more reformed beliefs imaged by the kind of conjugality implicit in the sonnet can be found in *De Doctrina,* bk. I, chap. 24 and its prooftexts, Romans 12 and 1 Corinthians 12, on the fellowship of the regenerate with each other and with the Father and the Son, "The Communion of Saints" *(sanctorum communionem)* of the Apostles' Creed (Yale Prose, 6:498). Citing Rom. 2:29, *De Doctrina* points out that this fellowship is "mystically one," not subject to space or time, and not contingent on the old law. The figures and images conveying the relationship are well-known—the church as a household becoming a temple (John 10:14, 10:16), the church as one flock protected and taught by Christ the shepherd (1 Peter 5:4), and as a spousal relationship (citing Rev. 19:7):

"Christ's love for this invisible and immaculate church of his is figured as the love of husband for wife. '*The marriage of the Lamb has come, and his wife has made herself ready*'" (Yale Prose, 6:500). Milton cites the figure in the divorce tracts: "Mariage, which is the neerest resemblance of our union with Christ." "Mariage is a solemn thing, som say a holy, the resemblance of Christ and his Church; and so indeed it is where the persons are truly religious; and wee know all Sacred things not perform'd sincerely as they ought, are no way acceptable to God in thir outward formality" (*Tetrachordon;* Yale Prose, 2:606, 630). The utility of the image, its conveying the doctrine of the communion of saints and the practice of marriage itself, is also evident in his description of the reformed church's discipline and rite in *The Reason of Church Government:*

> Againe, if Christ be the Churches husband, expecting her to be presented before him a pure unspotted virgin; in what could he shew his tender love to her more, then in prescribing his owne wayes which he best knew would be to the improvement of her health and beauty. . . . (Yale Prose, 1:755)

Also in *De Doctrina*, in a passage on "incomplete" and "complete" glorification, the believer's present, imperfect condition can anticipate his future, perfect sainthood and consummation, provided he continues in faith, love, and the testimony of the Spirit. The passage cites the "strong consolation" and hope of Heb. 6:18–23 that is not only "an anchor of the soul" but also that "entereth into that within the veil." We should therefore not forget that we are purged from our sins, and that we can "approach with a true heart, in full assurance of faith, having our hearts sprinkled from an evil conscience, and our bodies washed with pure water." It further cites 1 John 3:14 and 4:18: "'We know that we have passed from death unto life, because we love the brethren'; 'there is no fear in love, but perfect love casteth out fear'" (Yale Prose, 6:503–4, 630). "Complete," or perfect, glorification is of course a consummate vision, a seeing without veils, and might be tellingly compared to the husband's veiled "sight," which is suggested, or perhaps displaced unconsciously, by the espoused saint's veiled face:

> Complete glorification consists in eternal and utterly happy life, arising chiefly from the sight of God. It is described in Psal. xvi. 11: *you show me the path of life; that in your sight is an abundance of the most delightful joys; at your right hand eternally*, and xvii. 15: *in righteousness I will see your face; I will be satisfied with your likeness when I*

awake; . . . Matt. xiii. 43: *then the righteous will shine like the sun, in their Father's kingdom*, and xxii. 30: *they are as the angels of God in heaven*, and v. 8: *blessed are the pure in heart, for they will see God.* (Yale Prose, 6:630–31)

Complete glorification is also linked here to the spousal simile of Rev. 5:10 in which the new Jerusalem is figured, the holy city in the earlier context (citing Rev. 19:7) that is also the "invisible and immaculate church."

In the sonnet, the saint's bodily death occasions the hope for perfect glorification even within a context of delayed consummation. In the Christian tradition, of course, bodily death is first of all one punishment for sin. "That bodily death which precedes resurrection came about not naturally but through man's sin," *De Doctrina* declares, citing 1 Cor. 15:21 (Yale Prose, 6:399). Moreover, in what apparently develops the mortalist doctrine in the treatise, "the whole man dies," "body, spirit, and soul," because the whole man sins, not just the body. At the Second Coming, soul and body will be together received into heaven, but there is no "intermediate state," "no dwelling place in heaven even for the saints" until the Resurrection. As John 11:13 implies, "the soul of Lazarus was not called down from heaven . . . but was called up from the grave and awakened from the sleep of death" along with his body (Yale Prose, 6:400–406).

De Doctrina suggests, though, that this depressing truth for the living may not be perceived as such by the dead, as William Kerrigan has pointed out in his essay on Milton's mortalism.[7] All believers wish to be with Christ in heaven, to immediately experience complete glorification in heaven, as St. Paul longed to do. Even though the wish is strongly present, it does not logically follow that a soul immediately enters heaven (or hell). However, if "there is no time without motion," as Aristotle argued, "it is even more likely that, for those who have died, all intervening time will be as nothing, so that to them it will seem that they die and are with Christ at the same moment" (Yale Prose, 6:408–10). Hence, if there is an implicit mortalism in first comparing the espoused saint to one brought back from the grave, there is also in the dream a happy collapse of time in her "fancied" presence among the glorified in heaven—a heaven of the speaker's future, too, or one that is not in time at all. She is therefore both in the grave and in heaven simultaneously, as it were; she is the central and complementary image of the speaker's psychology, her presence incorporating both guilt and faith.

The Alcestis myth and the terms of purification in the old law, on the other hand, are similitudes soon qualified or denied because, again, they are inadequate frames for including simultaneous wishes for a punishing guilt and a redemptive faith. They allude to cultic resolutions of guilt, but they cannot convey actual atonement. The saint is not "pale and faint" like Alcestis when the comparison unfolds (line 4), and she is more than the old law provides: "*And* such, as yet once more I trust to have . . ." (line 7; emphasis added). Like the prescribed rites of the established church in England, mythology and the law are closed structures offering a facile, pseudoresolution to the speaker's spiritual development, and preventing the dialogic, ministerial opportunities of the saint's central context. Here, an intimate experience of the new covenant is conveyed with affective rather than prescribed authority:

> Love, sweetness, goodness in her person shin'd
> So clear, as in no face with more delight.
> But O as to imbrace me she enclin'd
> I wak'd, she fled, and day brought back my night.
>
> (lines 11–14)

"Full sight" (line 8) is therefore anticipated by actual rather than mythic or cultic emotion, by "Love, sweetness, goodness," and "delight" and not by the joy of Admetus (line 3) or by the wholesomeness of one "washt from spot" (line 5). Her delight, or the speaker's profound certainty of delight felt unconsciously and projected as her delight, is censored by the mixed emotions felt in early, gray light—the interjection "But O" suggesting both pain and delight in the speaker, an affective complexity. The mixed emotions then seem to fade into day, where they are resolved by the speaker's willful assertion, "night," his rhyme countering "sight" (line 10), "delight," and their illuminating pleasures.

The speaker's articulation of the Alcestis simile first hints at an emotional pattern of conscience impeding "Full sight" by allowing this assertive, self-protecting egoism. Looking at the simile more closely may further explain why it is invoked only to be contradicted by the less figurative radiance of the saint's love and sweetness—her unforced image that is clearly not pale and faint.

Hercules' rescue of Alcestis from death and his return of her to Admetus as a reward rather too neatly let one husband escape his guilt over participating in a death substitution. Accordingly, Alcestis's "pale and faint" presence cannot adequately answer, or express, the acute conscience of the

Christian husband. The Euripidean text itself may be construed as weak because it does not sustain the guilt of its characters. What dramatically could have been the reproachful presence of a wife and mother brought back is defused, at least in the Euripidean version, by the gradual recognition and welcome joy of Admetus, and by the conditional rite of purification Alcestis must undergo until "her obligations to the gods who live below / are washed away" by the third morning, when their reunion can be sexually consummated.[8] Admetus's courtesy to the gods and Hercules' generous response to his hospitality and to his devotion to Alcestis seem to conquer the initial moods of guilt and resentment.

The beginning of the play, on the other hand, emphasizes the stained moral psychology of rationalization. Apollo, angered at the murder of his son by one of Zeus's thunderbolts, has in turn killed the tenders of Zeus's fire. In punishment, Apollo must serve as a mortal for a time tending the oxen of his friend, Admetus. Because Admetus continued to revere Apollo's sacred prerogatives, the god persuades the Fates, Death, and "the lower powers" to accept a substitute to die in Admetus's place (*Alc.*, 11–14). The action begins after Admetus has asked his parents to die for him. Their refusal has prompted Alcestis's offer; she lies dying as Apollo declares, "The stain of death in this house must not be on me" (*Alc.*, 22). Apollo confronts Death, who has come to take Alcestis, and promises that Hercules will rescue her. Hercules "shall be entertained here in Admetus' house," he tells Death, "and he shall take the woman away from you by force, nor will you have our gratitude, but you shall still / be forced to do it" (*Alc.*, 68–70).

The mortal characters in the play do not trust or even know that this rescue has been promised. They lament their loss in contexts linking marriage with sacrificial death and the guilt of the survivor. Alcestis seems composed as she prepares for death by ritual bathing and by worshiping the hearth spirits (161-69). In her bedroom, however, as we hear from her maid, she weeps and addresses the symbol of her plight:

> O marriage bed
> it was here that I undressed my maidenhead and gave
> myself up to this husband for whose sake I die.
> Goodbye, I hold no grudge. But you have been my death
> and mine alone. I could not bear to play him false.
> I die. Some other woman will possess you now.
> She will not be better, but she might be happier.
>
> (*Alc.*, 176–82)

The maid appreciates what could have become the severe irony of Admetus's escape from death by Alcestis's sacrifice: "Had / he died, he would have lost her, but in this escape / he will keep the pain" (*Alc.,* 196–98). Perhaps trying to displace the pain and guilt already beginning, Admetus then implies that Alcestis is herself responsible for his grief, and that he is a victim:

> Before the gods, do not be so harsh
> as to leave me, leave your children forlorn.
> No, up, and fight it.
> There would be nothing left of me if you died.
> All rests in you, our life, our not
> having life. Your life is our worship.
>
> (*Alc.,* 275–80)

This complexity of love and blame is also felt by Alcestis, who replies,

> I put you first, and at the price of my own life
> made certain you would live and see the daylight. So
> I die, who did not have to die, because of you.
>
> (*Alc.,* 282–84)

Admetus accordingly agrees to her request not to marry again and not to give the children's care to a probably jealous stepmother (*Alc.,* 304–8). Alcestis will remain his bride even in death. He will pay his devotions to an image of her set in his bedroom and hold the cold image in his arms. Moreover, he hopes, she might come to visit him in his dreams and comfort him, "For they / who live find a time's sweetness in the visions of night" (*Alc.,* 355–56). Eventually, "I shall have them bury me in the same chest / as you, and lay me at your side, so that my heart / shall be against your heart" (*Alc.,* 365–67).

The complexity of love and guilt, of course, is not so easily resolved or romanticized, as Admetus's father, who had first been approached as a death substitute, angrily reminds him:

> You fought shamelessly for a way to escape death,
> and passed your proper moment, and are still alive
> because you killed her. Then, you wretch, you dare to call,
> me coward, when you let your woman outdare you,
> and die for her magnificent young man? I see.

> You have found a clever scheme by which you *never* will die.
> You will always persuade the wife you have at the time
> to die for you instead.
>
> <div align="right">(<i>Alc.</i>, 694–701)</div>

The play, then, certainly on one level, depicts a psychology of defilement, guilt, and resentment in its contexts of death by substitution as a consequence of intimacy. The play's at first rather sophisticated exposition of emotions resulting from love and leading to death, however, remains insufficiently edifying as a text for the sonnet's Christian speaker because of its simplistic and weak closure—its resolution in images of coital reunion, ritual sacrifice, and washing, and its resurrection from the grave as a reward for the good works of the husband. The sonnet's speaker, therefore, raises the specter of this carnal text as an initially pleasant wish granted to a "glad husband" (line 3) which then evolves into a simile of qualified disillusion, an Alcestis who is "pale and faint," a figure and a figurative rhetoric contrasting with the saint's shining communication of love and goodness.

As he recalls the dream encounter with his spouse, the speaker seems to turn away from the directness of her psychological presence and perhaps to employ the simile as a kind of boundary or protection against the transcendent authority her image may actually convey.[9] He is drawn to the mythographic simile in order to define the saint aesthetically rather than prophetically, which shifts his first intuition into conformity with prescribed learning. A more egoistic process, that of mythographic allusion, nearly impedes his heartfelt revelation of the Spirit. He is tempted to be a kind of Hercules bringing back another Alcestis by his own power, or perhaps to be an Admetus verbally forcing and recasting the saint's presence in another scenario of proposed images, thereby also accommodating his guilt in repeated dream encounters with his dead wife.

In the second quatrain, however, these egoistic and purgatorial assertions of control over the dead by the living are countered by an aura of the mystical body. Although the saint is somewhat like Alcestis rescued by force, she is more like one purified for entering or reentering a congregation: "Mine as whom washt from spot of child-bed taint / Purification in th' old law did save" (Sonnet XXIII, lines 5–6). She is perhaps most like a member of a church that exists simultaneously in the mind of the believer and in the fellowship of heaven in that she herself appears in both places. Here, the speaker's simile blends into direct statement and then into a declaration of faith. The saint's mystical church membership therefore complements a more authentic tone in his reaction to her, a tone comparable to attitudes implied in rightly reformed liturgy. The speaker now witnesses or testifies to his faith more directly; he does not read from or allude to a text prescribed for edification or for worship. He draws from the biblical promise alone, not so much as it may be printed for reading but as it lives in him as the heartfelt word: "as yet once more I trust to have / Full sight of her in heav'n without restraint" (lines 7–8). The declaration of faith rightly shifts the mythographic and Levitical dialogue between self and textual (or "constructed") heritage to a context of revealed, scriptural truth experienced prophetically. Having left a prescribed dialogue at the grave site, as it were, the witnessing husband enters a purified church along with the purified saint and meets a living, radiant memory of the word.

The rite of churching after childbirth as printed in the prayer book and practiced in the Anglican Church was of course criticized by some Puritans as both too Catholic and too Jewish, especially in its seemingly propitiatory offering of thanksgiving for the woman's rescue from death. This act, Thomas Cartwright argued, "of all other is most Jewish, and approacheth nearest to the Jewish purification, that she is commanded to offer accustomed offerings, wherein besides that the very word carried with it a strong scent and suspicion of a sacrifice." Further, "it cannot be without danger that the book maketh the custom of the popish church, which was so corrupt to be the rule and measure of this offering."[10] Cartwright also objects to the seemingly unholy banishment of the woman from church before her ritualistic return:

> The Churching of women: in which title [in the prayer book] yet kept there seemeth to be hid a great part of the Jewish purification: for like as in the old law she that had brought forth a child was holden unclean, until such time as she came to the temple to shew herself . . . so this term of churching can seem to import nothing else than a banishment, and as it were a certain excommunication from the Church during the space that is between the time of her delivery and of her coming unto the Church.[11]

More establishmentarian sources, such as Archbishop Whitgift, implied that, while "churching" may not be the best term for the practice, the rite was edifying in that it signified the consequences of original sin, and a deliverance from sin by references to birth and to the mother's escape from death:

The absence of the woman after her delivery is neither banishment nor excommunication, but a withdrawing of the party from the church by reason of that infirmity and danger that God hath laid upon womankind in punishment of the first sin, which danger she knoweth not whether she shall escape or no. . . . And this being done not Jewishly but Christianly, not of custom but of duty, not to make the act of lawful matrimony unclean but to give thanks to God for deliverance from so manifold perils.[12]

As we might expect, Milton, at least in his polemical writings, sees stupidity and spiritual danger in the ceremony and in its set language. In *An Apology for Smectymnuus*, he cites the "impertinences" of the prayer book text and the "dangers" of "set forms" in the liturgy, such "as those thanks in the womans Churching for her delivery from Sunburning and Moonblasting, as if she had bin travailing not in her bed, but in the deserts of *Arabia*."[13] A set form of churching, litanies, and the like may not only contain "errors, *tautologies*, impertinences," but also it "hinders piety rather than sets it forward, being more apt to weaken the spirituall faculties, if the people be not wean'd from it in due time" (Yale Prose, 1:937–39). The text itself is weak and cannot lend spiritual vitality to the believer:

And he who hath but read in good books of devotion and no more, cannot be either of eare or judgement unpractiz'd to distinguish what is grave, *patheticall*, devout, and what not, but will presently perceave this Liturgy all over in conception leane and dry, of affections empty and unmoving, of passion, or any heigth whereto the soule might soar upon the wings of zeale, destitute and barren. (Yale Prose, 1:938–39)

Puritan attitudes toward the prescribed rites of marriage and burial in the prayer book are similar. Some Puritans also objected to the delivering of funeral sermons by clergy at the grave site. Rather, the sermon should be delivered in the church after the burial.[14] Milton, too, objects to the prerogatives of the established church in the procedures of burial, attacking the "peculiar Simonie of our divines in *England* only," who take fees "for sacraments, marriages, burials, and especially for interring." Prayers at the grave site are but "superstitiously requir'd"; ministers should not "meddle" with marriages, which are civil contracts, even if "best, indeed, undertaken to religious ends." Parliament has rightly "recoverd the civil liberty of marriage" and "transferrd the ratifying and registring therof from the canonical shop to the proper cognisance of civil magistrates" (*Considerations Touching the Likeliest Means;* Yale Prose, 7:298–300).

Implicitly, then, removing marriage from the prescribed liturgy can encourage the spiritual development of the contracting parties by allowing the exercise of their Christian liberty. Their covenant is actually with each other and with God to be ratified by the community as a whole. The silent practice of Puritan burial also may imply a spiritual dialogue that is more heartfelt than institutional, as is perhaps indicated by Hooker's description of the early Puritan custom in his attempted rebuttal of it:

> But the greatest thing of all other about this duty of Christian burial is an outward testification of the hope which we have touching the resurrection of the dead. For which purpose let any man of reasonable judgment examine, whether it be more convenient for a company of men as it were in a dumb show to bring a corse to the place of burial, there to leave it covered with earth, and so end, or else to have the exequies devoutly performed with solemn recital of such lectures, psalms, and prayers, as are purposely framed for the stirring up of men's minds unto a careful consideration of their estate both here and hereafter.[15]

The importance of "careful consideration" transcends sectarian differences. Nonetheless, a devout Christian adhering to the reformed tradition might find a "solemn recital" "purposely framed" a facile resolution to this keen moment of grief, fear, and love when the opportunity for internal worship is so pronounced. Here an authoritarian celebrant and text might impede the essential religiosity of the event by their rhetorical aestheticism, making the Spirit's voice harder to hear and compromising the authoritative presence of the congregation. Stirring up the mind by prescribed texts is analogous to the impulse in the sonnet speaker to resolve the complex memory of the saint by first defining her image in terms of establishmentarian similes. However, the "dumb show" practice Hooker demeans is perhaps comparable to the sonnet's central portrait of the word not as an audible text but as a kind of presence—the speaker unconsciously attending the invisible church uniting him to his spouse in the dream.

The psychology of grief in the sonnet may seem problematic because it does not resolve the tensions of guilt and love, sin and forgiveness, in the speaker's waking life where day brings back night. The melancholy conclusion of the poem, however, undermines facile, perhaps establishmentarian, sanctimony, in order to leave us with a dialogic sense of the day and night internalized by the speaker. This dynamic relationship of moods expresses a more profound religiosity than could a peremptory, "solemn recital" of the promise of heaven at the end of the sonnet. The loss and longing, perhaps also the silence of internalized grief and prayer expressed by darkness, are nonetheless aspects of his dialogue with God and can also confirm his covenantal participation in the mystical body. The divine perspective itself seems to include a psychological dynamic of some kind even as it subsumes mortality and time—in *Paradise Lost*, "light and shade / Spring both" from God's mount (V.643–44). From his heavenly prospect, God beholds "past, present, future" (III.78), and in the heavenly community both good and evil are known (XI.251–52). The sonnet speaker implies he does not yet have this heavenly prospect or perspective consummately, although his faith approximates this point of view when his egoistic self sleeps and his profoundly loving self wakes during the dream.

In his discussion of the psychology and archetypes of sin in *The Symbolism of Evil*, Paul Ricoeur points out that the laments and condemnations characterizing prophetic writing in the Old Testament actually enhance their authors' experience of the covenant rather than detract from it. The lament concluding the sonnet and the motif of purification appearing or implied throughout it are also relatable to Ricoeur's interpretation of the paradoxes of emotion that underlie an intimate dialogue with God. Ricoeur notes that the alienation of the believer and its symbols of evil resulting from defilement, sin, and guilt can be experienced naively as cosmic hierophanies or, as we might expect, as "dream productions" that can be consistent with "the creativity of the poetic word."[16] Punishment proceeds initially from defilement, not from ethics. Purification rites associated with sexuality (marriage and, I would add, churching after childbirth) are prior to ethics and therefore somewhat ambiguous—they convey the threat of defilement by implying its possibility even as they grant exemptions from it.[17] When the dread of defilement is finally articulated verbally, an ethical experience or concept can result because defilement has then entered "the universe of the word" where pain and penance lead to order and happiness. The goal of this articulation, however, is not simply the removal of fear but the recasting of it "in a new range of feeling" such as one finds in the Hebraic covenant.[18] Eventually,

> the abolition of fear could only be the horizon, and, so to speak, the eschatological *future* of human morality. Before casting out fear, love transforms and transposes it. A conscience that is militant and not yet triumphant does not cease to discover ever sharper fears. The fear of not loving enough is the purest and worst of fears. It is the fear that the saints

know, the fear that love itself begets. And because man never loves enough,
it is not possible that the fear of not being loved enough in return should
be abolished. Only *perfect* love casts out fear.[19]

This dialectic, Ricoeur, continues, is "disconcerting" but also indicative of
humanity's fundamental relationship with and situation before God. Here
man "finds himself implicated in the initiative taken by . . . a god con-
cerned about man," an "initiative that calls and elects, appears suddenly
and becomes silent," and one signifying the "paradox of distance and presence" that is "at the heart of the consciousness of sin."[20]

In the sonnet, a similarly paradoxical initiative, or archetype, is imaged by the saint's presence and absence, and by the speaker's states of
consciousness. The speaker recalls that his spouse "fled" from his waking
state; consciousness and day seem to have repelled her. The speaker's de-
pression here is associated with her apparent fear, or her reluctance to complete her embrace of a conscious and perhaps conscience-stricken husband.
She inclines toward the speaker's less inhibited state of mind but flees from
his conflicted state. She represents his complex of desires for both purity
and punishment—her person and mind are "pure," untainted by childbirth
or death, but her flight as motion restarts his consciousness of time and
distance in that, again, there can be no time without motion. Day therefore
seems to enforce his evil conscience, the Adam-like conscience of a sinful
husband. Consummation at this time, the daytime clouded by self-abase-
ment, would dull the edge of the wife's mystical presence and absence, her
heavenly image reflecting his response to a mystical body transcending
established time and space. In the saint's flight, then, and in the speaker's
melancholic reaction, we may sense both a longing for a spiritual life without self-consciousness, a spouse and church subsuming guilt, and an inhib-
iting willfulness temporarily guarding the self from opening one's mind
and heart to grace and renovation.

We might again compare the married couple of *Paradise Lost* after
their love is also complicated by guilt. Their sexual encounter after the fall
is "the solace of thir sin" and "of thir mutual guilt the Seale" (IX.1043–44).
After they are "Oppress'd" by postcoital sleep, and "with conscious dreams
/ Encumberd," they wake with their eyes open, but with "thir minds / How
dark'ned; innocence, that as a veil / Had shadow'd them from knowing ill,
was gon" (IX.1045–55). The narrator regards this encounter as a seal or
sign of a degenerating moral attitude or psychology, and puns on the sacramental denotation of "Seale" as well as on its sexual reference.[21] "Loves

disport" (IX.1042) ironically cxprcsscs thcir guilt as a cucharistic parody, after they eat the fruit. Their seal of guilt is continuous with the "soild and staind" condition of their waking presence to each other and with the "signes / Of foul concupiscence" in their faces (IX.1076–78). The sexual act that once sealed original innocence and love, and that complemented their spontaneous, heartfelt liturgy of worship before the bower of their rest (IV.720–39), now signifies original sin.

For Adam, the guilt caused by less than perfect love leads to his wishing for darkness, a supposed security from heavenly faces and their brightness. His imagined security is also a punishment self-imposed, one selfishly protecting his ego's boundaries:

> O might I here
> In solitude live savage, in some glade
> Obscur'd, where highest Woods impenetrable
> To Starr or Sun-light, spread their umbrage broad
> And brown as Evening.
>
> (IX.1084–88)

Adam's wish for the experience of guilt without the possibility of dialogue, however, is prevented by Eve's attachment to him and by the more perfect judgment of the Son when he confronts them. Adam's lament is actually an address to Eve at first—"O *Eve*, in evil hour thou didst give ear" (IX.1067)— then becomes counsel not for a conditional "umbrage broad" but for "broad smooth Leaves" to cover their loins, so "that this new commer, Shame, / There sit not, and reproach us as unclean" (IX.1087–99). Later, in book X when the Son approaches them, "the voice of God they heard / Now walking in the Garden" (X.97–98), they hide themselves as sharing a mutual guilt: "they heard, / And from his presence hid themselves among / The thickest Trees, both Man and Wife" (X.99–101). At this time of judgment, "Love was not in thir looks, either to God / Or to each other, but apparent guilt, / And shame" (X.111–13). Nonetheless, their sealed mutuality ensures that a dialogue with God and their participating in the covenant and its promise continue. Their guilt as well as their love bind them to each other and to the Son, who has repeated his promise for atonement to the Father in heaven just prior to descending to judge them (X.68–84).

The spousal union of *Paradise Lost*'s mortal couple and their dialogic relationship with the Son allude to the true church and its future membership of Adam and Eve's descendants. The promise of atonement and reno-

vation and the contingency of the promise on their spousal union producing offspring qualify the tragedy of the epic's conclusion with a balancing
sense of love and providence (XII, 646-49). The melancholic tone of the
sonnet's concluding line has been balanced, though not overcome, by the
speaker's trust in a redeemed future for himself as well as for the saint. His
trust demonstrates his profound religiosity—an affection and faith possibly set against the feckless but authoritarian religiosity of a fallen church
and its liturgies of marriage, churching, and burial. The saint's presence,
unconsciously felt, better signifies the actual unity of Christians, living and
dead, with each other and with Christ. The Christian paradise promised by
the saint's inclining, however, is lost temporarily by the force of sinful
conscience in the speaker, the self-consciousness that protects an ego still
drawing authority from the old law rather than from the new.

The saint's near embrace of the speaker represents his wish for a consummation that is eschatological and ecclesiastical as well as sexual. In the
psychology of the dream, he cannot accept the embrace because it also
signifies an important cause of his guilt, the sexual encounter of a mortal
relationship that generated a child but also, like sin itself, generated death.
The saint's gesture is simultaneously a memory of love, sin, and death. Her
flight at day suggests that the speaker has heard a voice calling the ghostly
image of the saint back to the grave as well as the voice of heaven; the taint
of his sin is here censoriously present as the purity of a resurrected being.
This ambiguity and paradox nonetheless authenticate the speaker's theology of perfect love as a transcendence in his heart's core as well as in
heaven and beyond conscious understanding. But her disappearance is also
his wanting to flee from the dialogue of forgiveness and judgment, or to
flee from the nurturing aspect of a spiritual self subsuming both tainted and
pure, a loving yet concupiscent self whose wife dies in his place and then
returns as an image of greater, perfect love.

The essential Christianity possible in the mystical body, and which is
approximated by rightly reformed congregations of the visible church, dis-
solves the boundaries of the ego and teaches Christ's love for both the
living and the dead, the struggling sinner and the redeemed saint. The
chthonic superstition conveyed by "Joves great son" is therefore revealed
as mere text, as mythography or tragic drama defusing guilt and repentance. "Purification in th' old law" is also a merely textual rescue, a priestly
rather than Christological salvation. That which occurs in heaven, then,
may be the only salvation "without restraint." The saint's perfect love, or
the speaker's deep imagination of it, wishes to drive out fear and its resulting

aestheticism and superstition, but the imperfect love of the speaker's conscious life wishes to sustain a less threatening yet actually more benighted day of grief. The lover in the sonnet's day is not yet ready to forgive himself, and he presents his stubbornness as a weakness as well as a temporal limitation. He knows that a full sight of himself includes both the sinner and the saint, an Adam and his "Best Image," to cite *Paradise Lost* again (V.95), but he is not yet ready to give up his attachments to the waking world and its fallen structures.[22]

3

Sad Faith and
the Solitary Way

While Milton's polemical writings promote a dissenting, antiprelatical kind of Christianity, they also encourage a positive psychology of religion, one in which the "cultivation of devout affections" cooperates with "worship of the heart."[1] For the Independent Milton (and for many less-radical Protestants as well), true piety is first affectively experienced by the faithful. In a Pauline sense, they are linked to a loving Christ in mystical, invisible union and saintliness and perhaps in turn nurtured by a visible, congregational body modeled on the earliest Christian communities of Acts and the Epistles.

Milton's poetic voice also asserts an Independent ecclesiology and the priority of "devout affection" in the practice of worship, although most critics would agree that *Paradise Lost* eventually soars above seventeenth-century polemics in its depiction of Adam and Eve as the first congregation or as a typological figure of the church. Christopher Hill, for instance, locates the poem and Adam and Eve soberly, lovingly reunited in its last books within the historical context of defeat for the Good Old Cause of Puritanism, but as a nonetheless far-reaching narrative for the English people. Once the exiled couple "take their solitary way together," they are hopeful but represent a historical direction "far indeed from the Utopian enthusiasm with which Milton had greeted the Revolution in the early sixteen-forties."[2] Boyd Berry has also explained how specific allusions to Puritan controversial writing throughout *Paradise Lost* depart from as well as echo a rich tradition of Nonconformist discipline found in tracts and sermons.[3] Michael Lieb has noticed the mystical ecclesiology of the poem along with its archetypal images of the holy in the drama of mutual affection that ultimately refers the reader to an overriding, timeless theme of

God's transcendent love. As Lieb points out, the love of Christ binding the mystical body in the poem is "synonymous with none other than cultus."[4]

Such critical applications of cultural anthropology and of the historical record of dissent have led to valuable interpretations of the poem, and my comments on the poem's Puritan religiosity take these approaches into account. Perhaps more could be said, however, about some of the Congregational allusions of the poem's last books. In this essay, I would like to point out how its denouement of affective and spiritual renovation models ideal attitudes of worship for radically reformed and Independent congregations, whether of one Puritan household or many. As the narrative draws to a close, the shadowy yet certain prospect of losing their domain of Paradise affects the "adoration pure" of Adam and Eve and shifts their practice of worship, once "said unanimous" (IV.736–37), along with all their perception of divine truth, into a severe complexity of moods. Nevertheless, their tragic, prophetic knowledge influencing worship cooperates with generative affection and energy, states of mind and body once associated with the eroticized and unspoiled rites of love and worship in the bower of book IV. On the one hand, their now sober, reformed worship contrasts significantly with the adoration of unfallen minds, and of course with the carnal worship of fallen minds enthralled by appetite. On the other hand, beyond this sobriety, their reformed affection anticipates the sanctified discipline of Congregational nonconformity. Michael's tutelage of Adam and Eve in books XI and XII displays the tragedy of history, the consequences of their sin, but his shared prophecy, too, reforms the context of worship for the first congregation. In the process of this second, reformed instruction to Adam and Eve, Michael disarms Adam's liturgical prerogatives as patriarch and enables a more fruitful reaction to the "sad" future by both Adam and Eve, one that nurtures the Promised Seed. Mere lamentation, construed ironically in the narrative as sterile, displaced egoism, will then be subsumed by their joint celebration of a new covenant—the divine promise embodied in their relationship with each other and with the Savior.

In their "solitary" and reformed way, Adam and Eve are eventually a figure of the cause of the cultural malformation and of the mystical affection of the faithful transcending the tragedy of history. The figure's suggestion of an essential church completes Milton's characterization of "true religion" in the poem as devout affection better informed by an awareness of sin, and liberated by disestablishing vested oversight, or episcopacy. Their attaining a second Paradise, a place of "one Faith unanimous though sad" (XII.603), provides a mighty yet quiet defense against establishmentarian religion—a perennial, formidable avatar of the Great Adversary to be confronted by their progeny.[5]

In developing these points, I focus mainly on reformist allusions in passages of books XI and XII in *Paradise Lost;* I also refer to the scene of pure adoration in the bower of book IV and to the crisis of devout affection in book IX.

Reformed worship as a regenerative context begins just before Michael's descent in book XI, when Michael is instructed to inform Adam and Eve as well as to dismiss them from Paradise. Implicitly, this charge will lay new ground for grace to work. God observes them "soft'n'd and with tears" (XI.110), and tells Michael, "intermix / My Cov'nant in the womans seed renewd; / So send them forth though, sorrowing, yet in peace" (XI.115–17). This sad but fruitful mission is intuited affectively by them before it is expressed discursively:

> Mean while
> To resalute the World with sacred Light
> *Leucothea* wak'd, and with fresh dews imbalmd
> The Earth, when *Adam* and first Matron *Eve*
> Had ended now thir Orisons, and found
> Strength added from above, new hope to spring
> Out of despair, joy, but with fear yet linkt.
>
> (XI.133–39)

Here, the new context of their morning prayer signals right worship in the fallen world as a renovative mood expressed in fear as well as joy, or, as we hear Adam say to Michael a little later, as the intuition of limit that is felt simultaneously as tragic, a mood righteously obedient and rightly reasoned:

> if by prayer
> Incessant I could hope to change the will
> Of him who all things can, I would not cease
> To wearie him with the assiduous cries:
> But prayer against his absolute Decree
> No more avails then breath against the wind,
> Blown stifling back on him that breaths it forth:
> Therefore to his great bidding I submit.
>
> (XI.307–14)

Of course, Adam may yet be wrong about the effects of prayer. He has heard the decree of dismissal from the garden and reacted "at the newes /

Heart-strook with chilling gripe of sorrow"; Eve, similarly, "with audible lament" (XI.263–66). He has not heard the covenant of the Promised Seed unfolded in detail, and his understanding of Michael's first statement to him—"Heav'ns high behest no Preface needs: / Sufficient that thy Prayers are heard" (XI.251–52)—is incomplete, given what we have heard the Father say to Michael. Adam's grief and fear make up the moral psychology underlying his stoic tone. Understandably, he is trying to preserve dignity by self-pity, an affection that is based not so much on submission to God or to the decree as on his fear of death and of the unknown world outside Paradise. Prayer would be ineffective if prompted by this attitude, and his figurative closing off of authentic prayer ("breath against the winde, / Blown stifling back on him that breaths it forth") ironically communicates hostility and a resentment of truth. He will later see the breath of God inspiring history and conceiving the Redeemer. Adam's stoicism implies a kind of tragic knowledge, but a sadness contradicting an earlier speech to Eve when the results of his prayer of repentance seemed to include a more vital psychology:

> For since I saught
> By Prayer th'offended Deitie to appease,
> Kneel'd and before him humbl'd all my heart,
> Methought I saw him placable and mild,
> Bending his ear; perswasion in me grew
> That I was heard with favour; peace returnd
> Home to my brest, and to my memorie
> His promise, that thy Seed shall bruise our Foe;
> Which then not minded in dismay, yet now
> Assures me that the bitterness of death
> Is past, and we shall live.
>
> (XI.148–58)

This sentiment is more hopeful, of course. But, even though closer to the Christian vision of the narrator than the stoic passage, it too is somewhat wrongheaded, a wistful attitude toward the Father drawing the desolate reality of the fall back into the confines of the ego where the "bitterness of death" can be seemingly eased by a hierarchic imagination. To be sure, the lessening of bitterness is linked to repentance and the promise of the Seed, and his resignation later is rightly linked to the necessity of obedience. But his longing for a lost integrity in the security of an unfallen Paradise frames the doctrine of the promise too narrowly—it "now / Assures me that the bitterness of death / Is past, and we shall live." His praise for Eve that ends his speech is similarly compromised by his reestablishing prerogatives:

> Whence Hail to thee
> *Eve* rightly call'd, Mother of all Mankind,
> Mother of all things living, since by thee
> Man is to live, and all things live for Man.
>
> (XI.158–61)

While he rightly celebrates her carrying the Seed of Redemption (typologically he anticipates the Annunciation to Mary), his conclusion that eventually "all things live for Man" is a too-facile appreciation of the violent course of redemption, as he later learns from Michael.

Eve does not echo Adam's untutored enthusiasm here, but responds "with sad demeanour meek" (XI.162). She pictures a laborious existence for both of them, herself "deserving" a "Farr other name" than the source of life (XI.171), and concludes they could live intimately "content" in Paradise, "though in fall'n state" (XI.180). Her guilt is still continuous with her love for Adam and preserves her somewhat misinformed self-image as the authoress of death as well as the source of life. Her insight, too, has not yet been reformed by devout affection. Rather, at this point, the narrative voice authors the actual change Eve had unconsciously felt but attempted to qualify by romantic affection:

> So spake, so wish'd much-humbled *Eve*, but Fate
> Subscribed not; Nature first gave Signs, imprest
> On Bird, Beast, Air, Air suddenly eclips'd
> After short blush of Morn.
>
> (XI.181–84)

Before Michael's descent to earth, insight ("*Adams* eye") has been dimmed by "doubt / And carnal fear" (XI.211–12), but the authoritative signs reify the contending elements of moral psychology in the fallen world as well as demonstrate natural changes for the worse. "Heav'n by these mute signs in Nature" (XI.194) performs a kind of dumb show contradicting Eve's own wistful image of gentle decline, one anticipating the cosmic drama Michael later displays of "supernal Grace contending / With sinfulness of Men" (XI.359–60). Then, Adam will "learn / True patience, and to temper joy with fear / And pious sorrow," and thereby acquire equanimity in preparing for "Thy mortal passage of death" (XI.360–66). Both the symbolic and historical drama prompt a moral psychology in worship rather than merely establish a ritualistic mythology or mythography. The improved, more perceptive condition of mind accentuates the heritage of sinfulness yet also approaches a timelessness in levels of consciousness:

> Ascend
> This Hill; let *Eve* (for I have drencht her eyes)
> Here sleep below while thou to foresight wak'st,
> As once thou slepst, while Shee to life was formd.
>
> (XI.366–69)

Adam's foresight and Eve's prophetic association with the brooding power of the Spirit will not fully restore the mood of "adoration pure" enjoyed in the bower (IV.737), but the psychology will signify that of rightly reasoned worship in the microcosm of their marriage. Michael's removing Eve from the dialectic of reformation apparently does not lessen her prophetic authority, nor does it aggrandize Adam's patriarchy. Rather, she sleeps "As once thou slepst," one whose longing and dream fade not into nothingness or fear but into the real and the edifying.[6]

Their cooperative division of prophetic consciousness departs from the carnal affection and mutual sleep after their deluded satiety at the end of book IX and the "mutual accusation" of their next waking (IX.1034ff.), which is perhaps a figure of visibly degenerate, establishmentarian religion. That earlier context should be recalled to further explain the difference.

In the setting of hazardous dialogue completing the fall, Adam's affection for Eve is referred by him to "The link of Nature . . . Flesh of Flesh, / Bone of my Bone" (IX.914–15), a straitening, egoistic sense of the body of love. His narrowing vision of her presence, once his "Best Image of my self" (I.95), has been anticipated by Eve's metonymous transfer of her identity as worshiper to a fetishistic liturgy of the tree: "Not without Song, each Morning, and due praise / Shall tend thee, and the fertil burden ease . . ." (IX.799–801). Her "low Reverence don, as to the power / That dwelt within" (IX.835–36) not only alludes to carnal sacramentalism and superstition but also expresses the confused psychology of will-worship, her gesture demeaning what it intends to exalt in the worshiper and in the object of desire. Her resolved mutuality, "*Adam* shall share with me in bliss or woe" (IX.831), resonates with a demonic paradox of easing the tree's "fertile burden" while she grows "mature / In knowledge, as the Gods who all things know" (IX.801–3). At the same time, it contrasts with the right-minded worship, undefiled love, and the prophecy of issue once celebrated in the bower in book IV (lines 720–35). Adam's declaration, "for with thee / Certain my resolution is to Die" (IX.906–7), is also a degenerate courtliness, an exalted desire ironically travestying procreative love and worship.[7] The fruitless psychology of their naked vision after their carnal encounter—"thir Eyes how op'n'd, and thir minds / How dark'n'd" (IX.1053–54)—constrains what had been the time and the mood of their morning worship, and reduces the context of prayer to a savage and pathetic consciousness of pollution:

> But let us now, as in bad plight, devise
> What best may for the present serve to hide
> The Parts of each from other, that seem most
> To shame obnoxious. . . .
>
> (IX.1091–94)

The resulting "vain Covering" (IX.1113), the multifarious irony of the term inviting Milton's reader to distinguish pathetic guilt from edifying commemoration and repentance, is narratively developed as a chthonian fabrication, a mingling of egoistic and mythographic pastoralism with cowering uxoriousness. The fig leaves come from a "Mother Tree," whose "Pillard shade" and branches rooted again in the soil shelter a feckless herdsman, one sending "his pasturing Herds / At Loopholes out through thickest shade" (IX.1104–10). This is not an allusion to biblically antecedent flora, of course, as the narrator makes clear ("not that kind for Fruit renown'd" [IX.1101]), but a faithless kind of organicism, pastoral echoes of the allegorical figure of Sin and of the redundant energy of Pandemonium. Here, mutual devising impedes the fruitful remonstrance that can come from shame, and signifies "thir waste" (IX.1113) in distracting acts of selfish eroticism.

The confused, unproductive consciousness of shame Adam and Eve exhibit in coverings from the lesser fig tree is also "unlike / To that first naked Glorie" (IX.1114–15) radiating from the unfallen desire experienced in the bower and its open frame of right worship:

> Thus at thir shadie Lodge arriv'd, both stood,
> Both turnd, and under op'n Skie ador'd
> The God that made both Skie, Air, Earth and Heav'n
> Which they beheld. . . .
>
> (IV.720–23)

The mood of sabbatarian pastoral could have remained continuous with the image of God in humanity and with the Son's "Filial Power" (VII.587), as the angels' Sabbath hymn to the Father and his creation implies, celebrating a future "Race of Worshippers / Holy and just" (VII.630–31). In the fallen world, however, the "reward to rule / Over his Works" that was granted as appropriate to worshipers in God's image (VII.628–29) is mistaken as sanctioned prerogative and promiscuously mingled with patriarchal tyranny and egoism.

The prideful error of monarchs is uttered by Adam himself when he first reacts to the prospect of leaving behind important places of worship in Paradise he could have shown his sons (XI.319–21). Moreover, his visionary perception of exotic kingdoms, their races of worshipers ruled by "*Can*," "*Kings*," "*Mogul*," "*Ksar*," "Sultan," and "*Motezume*" (XI.388–411), suggests how lost and amazed a wayfaring Christian could become in confronting the spectacle of empire without the devout authority traced by "Our second *Adam* in the Wilderness," shown "all Earths Kingdomes and thir Glory" by the Tempter (XI.382–84). For visionary knowledge to be doctrinally fruitful, worthy to be passed on to progeny, Adam's "visual Nerve" must be "purg'd" from the effects of the "false Fruit that proms'd clearer sight" by medicinal herbs and by three drops from the Well of Life (XI.413–16).

A baptismal allusion is often noticed here, but the brightening of Adam's eye is probably intended to suggest a ministry of historical attentiveness more than the spiritual change implied in sacramentalism.[8] Catechetical attention, however, involves "the inmost seat of mental sight," a faculty reached by a kind of angelic, enforced sleep, his sinking into a trance and then being raised to attention by Michael:

> So deep the power of these Ingredients pierc'd,
> Eevn to the inmost seat of mental sight,
> That *Adam* now enforc't to close his eyes,
> Sunk down and all his Spirits became intranst;
> But him the gentle Angel by the hand
> Soon rais'd, and his attention thus recall'd.

$$(\text{XI.417–22})$$

For all Christians, of course, baptism itself may be figuratively as well as divinely construed. It is characterized as "a kind of symbol of our death, burial and resurrection with Christ" in *De Doctrina* (Yale Prose, 6:552), for example, and the devout affection characterized in the poetic figures of Adam and Michael involves the cooperation of several levels of perception. The angel's mystical vehicle for doctrine nurtures Adam's encounter with prophetic truth, from which he rises to a fruitful kind of discipline of conscience and consciousness. In the Calvinist tradition Milton follows, baptism is also an initiation into a covenant of grace continuous with Christ's atonement, one based on the internalization of conscience rather than on the law. The Mosaic law in its turn had been a type of baptism, as had Noah's ark, the pillar of cloud in the wilderness, and the crossing of the Red Sea (Yale Prose, 6:552, citing 1 Peter 3 and 1 Corinthians 10), images suggesting divine guidance and the preserving of cultural identity, but also, for Milton, the transitional structuralism of Judaism as an established religion. Perhaps more significantly for the poem's readership, the figurative imagination allows doctrine to abide independently yet viably, referring Christians to history yet freeing them from statist and establishmentarian appropriations of doctrine and discipline.

In the poem, Michael's catechizing of Adam and Adam's presumed communication to Eve, "at season fit," of what he has heard—"Chiefly what may concern her Faith to know, / The great deliverance by her Seed to come" (XII.597–600)—certainly derives from a paternal religiosity. Hence, the prospect of Eve's "meek submission" given to Adam by Michael (XII.597) could turn from confidence to egoism in the course of his instruction to her. This catechetical frame, however, is dissolved by the energy and authority of Eve's prophetic relationship with the Spirit, as if she were carrying not only the Promised Seed but also an independent perception better capable of appreciating the crucial psychology of the doctrine as devout affection. She is here discovered already awake by Adam, who had expected her to be asleep, and her confident tone can be related to her "gentle Dreams" (XII, 595) and the brooding power of the Spirit as well as to her love for Adam. To her, Adam is still "all things under Heav'n, all places" (XII, 618), a world that, like herself, is subordinate to heaven. Her courteous affection conveys a subordination of gender, to be sure, but also a sad unanimity in faith as well as in place, in that all orders of creation have been affected by sin. The poignant metonymy of places violated, lost, and regarded with fresh eyes as grounds for devotion and affection in the body of their love is also part of her sense of the Paradise within:

> with thee to goe,
> Is to stay here; without thee here to stay,

> Is to go hence unwilling; thou to mee
> Art all things under Heav'n, all places thou,
> Who for my wilful crime art banisht hence.
> This further consolation yet secure
> I carry hence; though all by mee is lost,
> Such favour I unworthie am voutsaft,
> By mee the Proms'd Seed shall all restore.
>
> (XII.615–23)

Eve's conclusion here invites us to recall the argument over safety and place in pastoral labor in book IX, and Adam's hazardous assertion of prerogative:

> But if thou think, trial unsought may finde
> Us both securer then thus warnd thou seemst,
> Go; for thy stay, not free, absents thee more;
> Go in thy native innocence, relie
> On what thou hast of vertue, summon all,
> For God towards thee hath done his part, do thine.
>
> (IX.370–75)

Then, as the discussion of their visible relationship and its protective discipline became quarrelsome instruction, Eve "thought / Less attributed to her Faith sincere" (IX.319–20), and a jealous self-esteem began to impede her appreciation of right worship. Succumbing to the serpent's promiscuous blandishments confusing eroticism and worship, Eve in her fallen state substituted possessive love for devout affection in her image of love's body: "Confirm'd then I resolve, / *Adam* shall share with me in bliss or woe" (IX.830–31). Now, the self-interest once displaced as desperate affection for Adam is subsumed by the confirmation of her faith in Adam and in God, a procreative relationship communicated by the prophetic imagination of dreams and witnessed by her as authoritative gospel. The sterile egoism of self-loathing consequent to narcissism, the faithless love she implicitly ascribes to "*Adam* wedded to another *Eve*," "A death to think," and the prospect of death as extinction (IX.828–30) had led her to design a marital relationship impeding both knowledge and repentance. This powerful psychology of fear and guilt is not dissolved by patriarchal dogmatism but by the experience of God in sleep. The goodness of the dream is immediately evident to her, and she does not need Adam's interpretation or reassurance as she did after recounting the satanic fantasy of book V. Then "she was cheard" by Adam's instruction, but still frail in "sweet remorse / And pious awe," afraid "to have offended" (V.129–35) rather than confirmed in faith.

The process of Adam's confirmation in faith is more episodic and retains a paternalistic transfer of authority in its management of biblical historicism. Michael's authority in transmitting the prophetic text and Adam's interpretive achievement are perhaps congregational models of necessary religion. The common denominator of both intuitive and discursive prophecy, however, is the devout affection nurturing unanimous faith, the mood of a communion of saints transcending the boundaries of heaven and earth, of angel and human, and, to some extent, of gender. Throughout Adam's "nobler sights" in books XI and XII, his dialogue with the angel is resolved in contexts preparing him for this mood and for a fit companionship with Eve, whose mystical perception of the gospel will complement his heritage of narrative.

Without devout affection in worship, religious authority can be confused with selfish rivalry, the context of the first murder. Cain's offering, "Uncull'd, as came to hand," is unacceptable because "not sincere." Abel's gift of the "best" of his flock, with "all due Rites" demonstrates that he is "More meek" (XI.435–44). Adam perceives the martyrdom of "that meek man," pious and pure in devotion (XI.451–52), but is further shocked in reflecting how this "first shape" of death may apply to him (XI.461–65). The legacy of will worship as death then expands to scenes of the lazaretto, where disease and deformity result from appetite, "th' inabstinence of *Eve*," essentially a lack of reverence for "Gods Image" in the self (XI.475–525). Even those taught by the Spirit will subordinate their gifts to carnality, and the seeming Sons of God in future generations will be "Destroyers rightlier call'd and Plagues of men" (XI.611–97).

Such establishmentarian models are opposed by the "example good" of the just man preaching, especially Noah (XI.809), whose building of the ark is also an admonitory sermon.[9] The ark itself and Noah's devotional attitude after the flood complement the "Cov'nant new" and its implied prophecy of timeless unity with God (XI.867). Both character and ministerial labor are vehicles for preserving the seed of righteousness, as Adam celebrates, a divine ethic eventually continuous with the Promised Seed. The flood removes Paradise along with all high places, "To teach thee," Michael explains, "that God attributes to place / No sanctitie" in itself (XI.836–37). Here Adam's pride of place in worship and in the issue with which he might have shared it is transformed into an image of abortive sterility—"an Iland salt and bare, / The haunt of Seales and Orcs, and Sea-mews clang" (XI.834–35). But envisioning the one just man whose prayer-ful gesture completes the rainbow's curve, Adam rejoices. His mood en-compasses the tragedy and approximates the angelic psychology and knowl-edge of his guide:

> O thou who future things canst represent
> As present, Heav'nly instructer, I revive
> At this last sight, assur'd that Man shall live
> With all the Creatures, and thir seed preserve
> Farr less I now lament for one whole World
> Of wicked Sons destroyd, then I rejoyce
> For one Man found so perfet and so just,
> That God voutsafes to raise another World
> From him, and all his anger to forget.
>
> (XI.870–78)

The patriarchy of devout affection, then, admonishes in order to nur-ture and to preserve the redemptive future. Its culture is ultimately an ex-pressive vehicle for sad and unanimous faith, a creative mood historically opposed by the patriarchy of mere place.

In book XII, the pseudopotency of displaced ego worship is over-whelmed by the valid nurturing of the seed in Abraham's entering into the covenant, his carrying the Promised Seed within the structure of national-ity. Nimrod, however, deviates from the postdeluvian, fecund heritage of "Labouring the soile, and reaping plenteous crop," when those fearing God rightly regard justice and "multiplie space," "Oft sacrificing Bullock, Lamb, or Kid, / With large Wine-offerings pour'd, and sacred Feast" (XII.15–21). The era emphatically "Under paternal rule" (XII.24) reduces procreative identity—the authority that should nurture—to monuments that merely externalize the ego, a phallicism or perhaps juvenile narcissism in keeping with Nimrod's arrogating "Dominion undeserv'd / Over his brethren" and with his hunting down men refusing "Subjection to his Empire tyrannous" (XII.26–32). These "builders" reconstruct chaos and Pandemonium, their external monument answered by a sterile vehicle of "hideous gabble" frus-trating an already misdirected sense of word, until, "all in rage, / As mockt they storm" (XII.56–58), their regressive infantile state is derided by heaven as low comedy and abhorred by Adam, "fatherly displeas'd" (XII.63).

Nimrod's betrayal of patriarchy and of the husbandry associated with

authorized worship is recognized by Adam as famished wretchedness, a
reality contradicting delusions of omnipotence (XII.72–78). A hell of erected
place, Nimrod's tyranny and vain edifice are in turn applied by Michael to
the moral psychology of right reason, to a mature perception of reality, if
also one hard to digest since the fall, or perhaps since Eve's hazardous
separation from Adam before the fall. A distorted echo of authorized procreation and patriarchy, and a reminder of Satan's degenerate relations and
issue, can be heard in Nimrod's begetting "Such trouble" on the quiet state
of men (XII.80–81), the fertile condition where liberty and reason could
have cooperated handsomely. Instead, "upstart Passions" are the issue of
"unworthie Powers" tyrannizing within and therefore constructing external thraldom (XII.88–91).

In the same context, Michael continues,

> Witness th' irreverent Son
> Of him who built the Ark, who for the shame
> Don to his Father, heard this heavie curse,
> *Servant of Servants*, on his vitious Race.

(XII.101–4)

Here the betrayal of devout affection is a sexual irreverence against the
prototype of covenant and husbandry. Ham's violation of a father's sacred-
ness demonstrates an egoistic obsession with secondary traits of potency,
and is consistent with the declining faculties of those who "forsake the
living God, and fall / To worship thir own work in Wood and Stone / For
Gods!" (XII.118–19).

However, Abraham's renovation of devout patriarchy, after he was
"Bred up in Idol-worship" (XII.115), eventuates in the proliferating of righteous seed. God calls him "by Vision from his Fathers house, / His kindred
and false Gods, into a Land / Which he will shew him, and from him will
raise / A mightie Nation" (XII.121–24), and "A Nation from one faithful
man to spring" (XII.113). He is freed by the covenant from those worshiping "thir own work in Wood and Stone" just as Eve was once freed from
self-absorption, heeding the promise of a reality of place with Adam, "the
Patriarch of mankind" (V.506):

> where no shadow staies
> Thy coming, and thy soft imbraces, hee
> Whose image thou art, him thou shall enjoy

> Inseparablie thine, to him shalt bear
> Multitudes like thy self, and thence be call'd
> Mother of human Race.
>
> (IV.470–75)

The Exodus event is similarly fruitful in its issue, and also bred from a context narrating deliverance from inauthentic patriarchy, that of Pharaoh's tyrannic rule seeking "To stop thir overgrowth, as inmate guests / Too numerous; whence of guests he makes them slaves" (XII.166–67). His presumed idolatry and his infanticide of male issue objectify the moral psychology of his "rage" and "stubborn heart, . . . still as Ice / More hard'n'd after thaw" (XII.193–94). The authentic patriarchy of Moses cooperates in deliverance of the seed and gives shape to salvation by his following God's command, just as he structures the chaotic, formlessly appetitive waves: "two christal walls, / Aw'd by the rod of *Moses* so to stand / Divided, till his rescu'd gain thir shoar" (XII.197–99). Here the vertical imagery conveys not the disorder of pride in place but God's "wondrous power" that He "to His Saint will lend," a just potency and guiding authority magnified in the cloud and pillar of fire (XII.200–204), authority repeated in the inundation of Pharaoh's host, "when by command / *Moses* once more his potent rod extends / Over the Sea; the Sea his Rod obeys" (XII.210–12), and finally issuing in the law and ordered ritual, "types" of the Promised Seed (XII.232–33).

Nurturing the Promised Seed by preserving national structure is simultaneous with "informing" by narrative, legal, and ceremonial texts (XII.233). Ceremony, however, loses authenticity when the chosen nation is confronted with the Incarnation mystery and the doctrine of justification by faith. Adam at this point demurs at the seeming cumbersomeness of the law among the chosen seed: "So many Laws argue so many sins / Among them; how can God with such reside?" (XII.283–84), and, while continuing to illustrate the contention of grace and sinfulness, Michael denigrates the sacrificial efficacy of ceremony: "Law can discover sin, but not remove." However, "shadowie expiations weak, / The bloud of Bulls and Goats" can dramatize, or figure, that "Some bloud more precious must be paid for Man, / Just for unjust" (XII.290–94). Further, "a better Cov'nant, disciplin'd / From shadowie Types to Truth, from Flesh to Spirit," is needed in order "to free / Acceptance of large Grace, from servil fear / To filial, works of Law to works of Faith" (XII.303–6).

This better covenant is a more securely articulated structure than ritual

drama, one both loving and fruitfully mysterious, like the prior union of
the Father and Son or perhaps that of unfallen Adam and Eve—not "servil
fear" but "filial," a pastoral, nurturing text referring humankind to the bower.
The return to the garden by covenant is here implicit in Joshua, "whom the
Gentiles *Jesus* call," leading his people home, as the incarnate Son will
later "bring back / Through the worlds wilderness long wanderd man / Safe
to eternal Paradise of rest" (XII.312–14). But, rest is again impeded by the
displaced vanity of those pretending to guard religion. They apprehend
little beyond the emblems of secular power, and separate by strife the force
of authority from its nurturing aspect:

> But first among the Priests dissension springs,
> Men who attend the Altar, and should most
> Endeavour Peace: thir strife pollution brings
> Upon the Temple it self: at last they seise
> The Scepter, and regard not *Davids* Sons,
> Then loose it to a stranger, that the true
> Annointed King *Messiah* might be born
> Barr'd of his right.
>
> (XII.353–60)

This fruitless solemnity among the priests is countered by an authentic
solemnity, a powerful and yet accessible emblem conveying the good news
of Jesus' birth. A star "proclaims him com," "And guides the Eastern Sages,"
while "His place of birth a solemn Angel tells / To simple Shepherds" and
"a Quire / Of squadrond Angels" sings (XII.361–67). Patriarchy here is
both pastoral and sublime, as the context shifts from narrative to prophetic
utterance and frames the doctrine of the Incarnation:

> A Virgin is his Mother, but his Sire
> The Power of the most High; he shall ascend
> The Throne hereditarie, and bound his Reign
> With earths wide bounds, his glory with the Heav'ns.
>
> (XII.368–71)

Adam's understanding of a truly devout fatherhood deepens, and he
intuits the cooperative relation between husbanding rites mysterious in
wedded love and the uniting of God with mankind. Michael's prophecy
then prompts a spiritual and emotional catharsis, words now "breathd" as
authenticated signs of renovation in Adam's moral psychology:

He ceas'd, discerning *Adam* with such joy
Surcharg'd as had like grief bin dew'd in tears,
Without the vent of words, which these he breath'd.
    O Prophet of glad tidings, finisher
Of utmost hope! now clear I understand
What oft my steddiest thoughts have searcht in vain,
Why our great expectation should be call'd
The seed of Woman: Virgin Mother, Hail,
High in the love of Heav'n, yet from my Loyns
Thou shalt proceed, and from thy Womb the Son
Of God most High; so God with man unites.

                          (XII.372–82)

      Although he comprehends the essential doctrine, Adam seems to expect that eschatology will continue as dramatic narrative:

Needs must the Serpent now his capital bruise
Expect with mortal pain: say where and when
Thir fight, what stroke shall bruise the Victors heel.

                          (XII.383–85)

Michael again corrects the reading, drawing Adam's attention to the doctrinal significance of the Atonement, Resurrection, and Second Coming (XII.404–65). Adam wants to know "where and when" the Victor will fight the serpent, after God unites with man, but Michael replies, "Dream not of thir fight, / As of a Duel, . . . / . . . not therefore joynes the Son / Manhood to God-head, with more strength to foil / Thy enemie" (XII.386–89). His emphasis internalizes doctrine as a complement to emotional and spiritual recovery, and therefore conditions Adam's understanding of the covenant as affection. Adam's issue will be redeemed "Not by destroying *Satan*," Michael explains, "but his works / In thee and in thy Seed" (XII.394–95). The Victor will fulfill God's law, "Both by obedience and by love, though love / Alone fulfill the Law" (XII.403–4). This new sense of the covenant makes the following accelerated narrative of the New Testament an affective experience for Adam rather than a sermon preached without a right frame of mind in its auditor, or a merely external display of authority. In time, "Salvation shall be Preacht" "Not onely to the Sons of *Abrahams* Loins / . . . but to the Sons / Of *Abrahams* Faith wherever through the world; / So in his seed all Nations shall be blest" (XII.446–50). The faithful will be baptized as

the signe
Of washing them from guilt of sin to Life
Pure, and in mind prepar'd, if so befall,
For death, like that which the redeemer dy'd.

(XII.442–45)

A mind so prepared is mystically linked to the Resurrection and the fall rather than merely resigned to dissolution, and will appreciate the blessing of Abraham's seed through the preaching of the word to nations rather than in filial power alone. National identity will serve the purposes of faith and contain the word in the course of history. Baptism will be an expressive act with affective resonance, and preaching an evangelical proliferating of authority. Adam's enthusiastic tone complements this fecundity of spirit in prophecy:

O goodness infinite, goodness immense!
That all this good of evil shall produce,
And evil turn to good; more wonderful
Then that which by creation first brought forth
Light out of darkness! full of doubt I stand,
Whether I should repent me now of sin
By mee done and occasiond, or rejoyce
Much more, that much more good thereof shall spring,
To God more glory, more good will to Men
From God, and over wrauth grace shall abound.

(XII.469–78)

Seeming to feel the moving of the spirit as an emotional and divine force, Adam can regard himself in a heroic posture: "full of doubt I stand"— "doubt" indicating his perception of limit, the reality of cognitive understanding as incomplete, yet "stand" signifying his moral satisfaction and intentionality, his creative and brave personality resulting from the Spirit's moving across the abyss of a darkened conscience, the "Abyss of fears" he once lamented in his address to conscience as he lay on the ground cursing his creation (X.842). Michael's description of the Comforter enhances the role of the Spirit as a guiding, internal doctrine, one proliferating as a ministry of the word as well as the particular renovation of Adam (XII.485–507).

Opposed to the ministry of the heartfelt Law of Faith, the evangelical gifts of "all Tongues," the tidings, doctrine, and "story written" (XII.502–6) are the "grievous Wolves" (XII.509) of a clerical establishment,

> Who all the sacred mysteries of Heav'n
> To thir own vile advantages shall turn
> Of lucre and ambition, and the truth
> With superstitions and traditions taint,
> Left onely in those written Records pure,
> Though not but by the Spirit understood.

(XII.510–15)

The defacing assault on the "written Records pure" is consistent with the violation of conscience, the imagery suggesting vicious sexual assault, perhaps recalling Eve's dream, or Adam's seizing Eve's hand after the fall. Overreaching clerics will appropriate the Spirit to themselves,

> and from that pretense
> Spiritual Laws by carnal power shall force
> On every conscience; Laws which none shall finde
> Left them inrould, or what the Spirit within
> Shall on the heart engrave. What will they then
> But force the Spirit of Grace it self, and bind
> His consort Libertie; what but unbuild
> His living Temples, built by Faith to stand.

(XII.520–27)

One result of their assault is the error that religion can be satisfied "in outward Rites and specious formes," while those "who in the worship persevere / Of Spirit and Truth" suffer persecution (XII.532–35). The final renovation of the eventually "perverted World" (XII.547), however, is not broodingly sexual and spiritually nurtured so much as asexual, phoenixlike, and violent, and the narrative turns apocalyptic. "The Womans seed, obscurely then foretold, / Now amplier known thy Saviour and thy Lord" (XII.543–44), returns,

> In glory of the Father, to dissolve
> *Satan* with his perverted World, then raise
> From the conflagrant mass, purg'd and refin'd,
> New Heav'ns, new Earth, Ages of endless date
> Founded in righteousness and peace and love,
> To bring forth fruits Joy and eternal Bliss.

(XII.546–51)

The angelic mood here is gloriously cataclysmic in order to enforce Michael's loathing for those who impede the force of conscience and obscure "those written Records pure" by arrogating the Spirit's efficacy in worship to themselves.

The issuing of "fruits Joy and eternal Bliss" is anticipated by a gentler mood of Adam's possessing "A Paradise within thee, happier farr" than "this Paradise" (XII.586–87), and is the cumulative result of adding deeds to knowledge, a dialectical breeding of an integrated personality animated by love. Even though Adam might consider apprehending "All secrets of the deep, all Natures works," Michael explains, and enjoy "all the rule, one Empire" (XII.578–81), his learning about the Redeemer's example of trusting providence, "Subverting worldly strong, and worldly wise / By simply meek" (XII.569–70) is "the sum / Of wisdom" (XII.575). The sum is cognitive doctrine as well as affection, the unanimous intellection attained by attending to the Gospel narrative rather than by projecting or establishing new dominions.

The fruit of joining "Vertue" and "Deeds" to this high wisdom is now engendered, but also not bound by gender. The nurturing role of charity is now coterminous with its roles as animating force and structuring principle:

> onely add
> Deeds to thy knowledge answerable, add Faith,
> Add Vertue, Patience, Temperance, add Love,
> By name to come call'd Charitle, the soul
> Of all the rest.
>
> (XII.581–85)

Adam's sharing of the Gospel text with Eve is continuous with their new or reformed generative relationship, and their minds and bodies nurture the promise and the Promised Seed. The imagined context for their joining in knowledge and love is also liturgical, suggesting a mood of reformed, eucharistic worship, their unanimous faith articulated by meditation on the Redemption. "At season fit" (XII.597), Adam should share the word with Eve, although in a sadder tone than that of their first encounter in the bower.

Eve's wakeful greeting of Adam after he has heard Michael, her words "not sad" (XII.609), is the new covenant greeting the old. Her risen state and enthusiastic consciousness of history is an equivalent, if antinomian, authority. The resulting heritage of sad, unanimous faith, "With cause for evils past, yet much more cheer'd / With meditation on the happie end" (XII.603–5), is encouraged by the excluding angel, an image of authority who disestablishes yet one fairly taking Adam and Eve "In either hand" before disappearing (XII.637–40). This newly enlightened marriage and its heavenly guide embody the reformed and essential church, the ark in which devout affection is carried.

4

The Unobserved
Kingdom

In *Paradise Regain'd*, the Son redeems a realm of knowledge for human-kind, states of mind long tyrannized by satanic delusion and vanity, and by egoistic appetites masked as statecraft, academic prowess, and aestheti-cism. In turn, by locating the Savior's heroic labor in a cultural as well as spatial wilderness, Milton implicitly encourages a truly informed, or re-formed, interpretation of the later, more significantly doctrinal events in the New Testament itself—the Son's atonement for sinful, alienated de-scendants of Adam and Eve, and his Resurrection as a victorious promise of new, eternal life. Important, too, for the work's first readers, but not, I believe, sufficiently explained by its modern critics, is Milton's associating a reformist sense of the body of the church with his hero's ethical and psychological merits. In this essay, I would like to discuss how the Son's regaining a kingdom both "Real" and "Allegoric," rather than a kingdom presumably either "Real or Allegoric," as in Satan's thinking (*P.R.,* IV.390), is not only a transcendent epistemology but also an ecclesiastic heritage superior to an establishmentarian, prelatical church. More specifically, I would like to draw attention to ways in which the Son's kingdom in the poem, like Milton's characterization of the Son himself, suggests the ide-als of Puritan congregations.[1]

To be sure, the Son and Satan battle for all souls and minds and for dominion over a fallen or a redeemed world. In another sense, they con-tend for a kingdom issuing from the hero's intimate communion with the Spirit in the wilderness, that of the mystical body underlying true, reformed religion. The Son's heroic labor in the wilderness begets a subjective yet congregational kingdom of interpretive authority and right worship for the faithful. The physical body of Jesus in the poem begins to imply the meton-ymous, mystical body of Christ, as the Son embarks on enacting the Father's "solemn message" of salvation recalled in the poem's first book (I.135). In the last book, when the Son stands confidently and independently in his attitude toward the establishmentarian tendency of the old law, he is a figure of the sanctified body proclaiming saving doctrine, amazing a rightly excommunicated adversary and defending the faithful congregation who await his return. Similarly, the poem's allusions to the congregational seals of baptism and the Lord's Supper suggest sanctified membership in the essential church as a state of mature witness and fruitful worship, traits of right-minded congregations whose liturgy is heartfelt rather than prescribed or overseen. These aspects of Puritan ecclesiology, then, contribute significantly to the poem's theme of recovered Paradise. My discussion of them centers around the images of reformed sacramentalism and pastoral discipline in each of the poem's four books.

For many reformers, Milton included, baptism would not be regarded as a sacramental initiation alone. Rightly practiced, it is a figure of mature professions of repentant faith by those cognitively aware of their heritage of sin. In the poem, John the Baptist first proclaims "Repentance" to the faithful as their common ground, and, simultaneously, "Heavens Kingdom nigh at hand / To all Baptiz'd," when "flock'd / With aw the Regions round" (I.20–22). He is a model of the pastor who should be allied intuitively, congregationally, with the Savior and with the faithful, and he aims his preaching toward repentance and prophetic recognition. For him, pastoral hierarchy is most fully realized when it is resigned to the mystical head of the congregation and simultaneously applied to promulgating saving doctrine: "[He] witness bore / As to his worthier, and would have resign'd / To him his Heav'nly Office" (I.26–28). The doctrinal efficacy of John's baptizing is soon confirmed by the Father, the terms here perhaps alluding to a reformist emphasis on magisterial consensus and approval as the proper function of the seal of confirmation—for reformers, a continuation of baptism.[2]

> nor was long
> His witness unconfirm'd: on him baptiz'd
> Heav'n open'd, and in likeness of a Dove
> The Spirit descended, while the Fathers voice
> From Heav'n pronounc'd him his beloved Son.
>
> (I.28–32)

The iconography is hierarchic, to be sure, but cooperative with John's sincere humility and his doctrinally fruitful submission to the truth. Satan, on the other hand, "At that assembly fam'd / Would not be last" (I.33–35).

His leadership and supposed prerogatives are threatened by models of the true pastorate and by the leveling prospect of an unlocalized, pervasive kind of authority. His initially intuitive reactions of "wonder," "envy," and "rage" (I.38) ironically result in the absurdly cognitive delay of a council in hell, where a perverse dialecticism and hermeneutics are structured like Pandemonium itself as a sanctuary against the Father's penetrating voice. For the reader, Satan's "ill news" (I.64) reflects John's good news, but in Satan's pastorate truth is resisted by obscurantism or temporarily evaded by searching for merely categorical definition. When he recalls the prophecy of the Seed who would wound his head, he pretends to have the welfare of his own flock in mind—"our freedom and our being / In this fair Empire won of Earth and Air" (I.62–63). But, the empire is a solipsistic vision now threatened by the actual, by the awesome truth he is doomed to face even as his oratory would lessen the impact of prophetic meaning: "by the head / Broken be not intended all our power / To be infring'd" (I.60–62). The Seed's "birth to our just fear" was first cause for some alarm, Satan continues, and now his "full flowr, displaying / All vertue, grace and wisdom to achieve / Things highest, greatest, multiplies my fear" (I.66–69). The figures of seed, birth, and full flowering undermine his rhetorical intention, and as a poetic good news they enhance the generative associations of Heaven's opening at the Jordan and the Spirit's descending "in likeness of a Dove" (I.30) just witnessed. Moreover, for many readers, the Spirit as dove would recall not only the "Dove-like" Spirit of *Paradise Lost*, "brooding" generatively over the "vast Abyss" of the potential cosmos, but also the Spirit's influence over that epic narrator's prophetic and repentant psychology: "What in me is dark / Illumin, what is low raise and support" (I.21–23). In *Paradise Regain'd*, the Spirit "With prosperous wing full summ'd to tell of deeds / Above Heroic, though in secret done" (I.14–15) engenders the evangelistic or gospeller side of the poet along with the new cosmos possible in the new abyss, the second Eden to be "rais'd" in the "wast Wilderness" where Jesus has been led by the Spirit, and where the Tempter is to be "foil'd / In all his wiles" (I.5–8).

For Satan, the Spirit's presence necessitates "wiles," a rhetorical desert of false flowers. His own usage of "prosperous," an epic memory of the "dismal expedition" across the first abyss, is another effort to shore up an ego threatened by plain truth:

> I, when no other durst, sole undertook
> The dismal expedition to find out
> And ruin *Adam*, and th'exploit perform'd

Successfully; a calmer voyage now
Will waft me; and the way found prosperous once
Induces best to hope of like success.

(I.100–105)

While the event for John the Baptist signifies divine and earthly identity, fruitful repentance, and the kingdom near at hand, it also dramatically
portrays the excommunicated mind of one still rejecting the hierarchy of
spiritual merit. Satan's ironic role of champion and seducer, his heroic ethos
couched in the rhetoric of "I, "no other durst," and "sole," then magnified
by the sexual connotation of "ruin" and "exploit perform'd," both masks
and reveals his lurid confusion of loathing and desire in regarding the Son,
here contextually displaced by Adam and, implicitly, by Eve. As in the first
epic, he would violate rather than long contemplate mysterious innocence,
and thereby eclipse his consciousness of a second Eden, the Son's fruitful
union with the Father and with humanity.

The Father's speech to Gabriel immediately following depicts an unimpeded ethos of procreative authority and heroism. Unlike that of the
consistory's "great Dictator" (I.113), the Father's attitude is "to verifie that
solemn message" of the Annunciation to Mary (I.133). The speech derives
from the eternal knowledge coterminous with absolute truth and with the
generation of eternal truth in the world's time by means of the second Eve.
Satan's position of seeing the truth desperately, outside of, or excommunicated from, the truth as a state of existence again makes him an "unweeting"
participant in the Father's will (I.126). The Father's verification of prophecy to his heavenly audience also recalls the brooding presence of the Spirit
encountered by the Virgin and, indirectly, the recent event at the Jordan
displaying the Sonship of the mature Jesus:

Then toldst her doubting how these things could be
To her a Virgin, that on her should come
The Holy Ghost, and the power of the highest
O'er-shadow her: this man born and now up-grown
To shew him worthy of his birth divine
And high prediction, henceforth I expose
To Satan.

(I.137–43)

The present maturity of the Virgin's Son cooperates with the verbal maturing, as it were, of "that solemn message" and the "high prediction" of proph-

ecy before the Son's pastoral life in the world. This verification confirms that truth is full-grown, stalwart against Satan's regressive, serpentine "utmost subtilty" (I.144) and "fallacy" that had surprised Adam (I.155).

For many Protestants, sacramental baptism itself was and is a cognitive as well as spiritual kind of initiation intended for mature Christians. As a seal of spiritual growth, it is inappropriate for infants. This emphasis on the mature Christian's experience of baptism is consistent with the identity of the Son in the poem and, further, with the narrative's implication of both the prophetic word and the person of the Word as fulfilled or complete in the Gospel and in history. *De Doctrina* argues, "How can infants who do not understand a word, be purified by the word [i.e., by baptism]? It means as much to them, as it does to an adult to hear an unknown language. For we are not saved by that outward baptism which washes away merely the filth of the flesh, but as Peter says, *by the obligation of a good conscience,* and conscience is not a property of infants" (Yale Prose, 6:545). Such definitions of baptism also imply a conscious, mature commitment to membership in the mystical body—a pledge to purity in life, regeneration through the Holy Spirit, and union with Christ. In the reformed sense of baptism, "we are initiated into the gospel, which is a rational, manly, and utterly free service. Under the law men were not only born infants, they grew old as infants; but under the gospel and baptism we are born men." A mature appreciation of the Gospel is also implied by having the administrator of the seal be a preacher of the Gospel, or at least a well-informed believer (Yale Prose, 6:544, 548).

Baptism as practiced by John signified repentance by ritual washing. Reformed Christian baptism requires not only repentance but also knowledge and faith in the believer who is to be joined to Christ, a union better signified by immersion than by a mere sprinkling of water. John's baptism of repentance and of faith was based on a partial revelation of Christ, but later the rite could be founded on faith in a Savior. The exceptional instance of Christ's baptism at the Jordan, however, was mainly to witness the Son of God. The poem, of course, alludes to several kinds of baptism in Scripture— John's baptism of repentance, John's baptism of Jesus as a witnessing testament, and the later baptism sanctioned by Christ to confer the Holy Spirit and to establish our union with him in death and resurrection. Both saving doctrine and right-minded church discipline derive from all three kinds.

Such emphasis on a mature experience of baptism and its reformed practice as analogous to the Christian's repudiation of the old law (or its remnants in the rituals and prerogatives of the established church) can be further related to the dramatic situation of the poem. The "manly" event of baptism, a free initiation into the Gospel and one contradicting the spiritual infancy of the old law, is itself an appropriately heroic action for the Son. Even the "weakest Christian," Milton comments in *The Reason of Church Government*, is one who has "thrown off the robes of his minority, and is a perfect man, as to legal rites." Here he observes that such practices as crossing the infant's head with oil after baptism implicitly declare institutional rubrics to be as important as God's will. More dangerously. the established approach to ritual would "stifle the sincerity of our new cov'nant," and confuse the "simplicity of doctrine" with "the wisdom of the world" and thereby lessen the authority of the truth (Yale Prose, 1:828–29). Perhaps, too, Milton suggests something nearly satanic in the bishops' subordination of the "unexpressible Image of God the father" in their "dark overcasting of superstitious coaps and flaminical vestures" during the rite (Yale Prose, 1:827–28). In *Paradise Regain'd*, Satan strives for a similar confusion between the new covenant and the wisdom of the world in his tempting the Son with promises of political and academic grandeur after intuiting the authority signified by the baptismal event at the Jordan. Like the prelatical establishment, his willful, self-serving complication of the event's directness is a displaced egoism. His intelligence, like the "fleshly pride and wisdom" of the bishops in their comprehension of ceremony, also obscures "the pure simplicity of saving truth." (Yale Prose, 1:827).

Once baptized, the Son moves farther into the wilderness to consider "How best" and "which way first" he should "Publish his God-like office now mature" (*P.R.*, I.185–87). The Father has told Gabriel that the hero is already "This perfect Man, by merit call'd my Son" (I.166), and the pastoral and redemptive life that will verify this "solemn message" will be preceded here by "the rudiments / Of his great warfare" with Satan, Sin, and Death. The rudiments will include "Humiliation and strong Sufferance," a paradoxical "weakness" that is also "consummate vertue" able to conquer "cunning," "Satanic strength / And all the world, and mass of sinful flesh" (I.145–66). Implicitly, the rudiments will also be a groundwork for the mystical body of Christ as a congregation—the "Angels and Aetherial Powers, . . . now," and the "men hereafter" who "may discern" this perfect Man's consummate virtue and his purpose "To earn Salvation for the Sons of men" (I.163–67). The angelic choir reacts first to the Father's word as prophecy and dictum, admiring silently and then by celebratory hymns. Their celestial corporality and voices cooperate lyrically and affectively in communicating the redemption of minds and hearts:

> the hand
> Sung with the voice, and this the argument.
>   Victory and Triumph to the Son of God
> Now entring his great duel, not of arms,
> But to vanquish by wisdom hellish wiles.
> The Father knows the Son; therefore secure
> Ventures his filial Vertue, though untri'd.
>
> (I.171–77)

The harmony of hand and voice is also a right-minded discipline, one choreographing both understanding and affection spontaneously. This kind of worship also heralds the reformed liturgy of congregations "hereafter," a prophetic and liturgically reformed argument in contrast to the pseudodialectic and responsories of Satan's consistory.

When the Son recalls the baptism, he displays a consciousness already accomplished in mature witness of the inspired truth, a mind rightly linking "message" to solemnity. "I consider / What from within I feel my self, and hear" (I.197–98), he declares authoritatively, while yet discerning that his "present state" is "ill sorting" with "What from without comes often to my ears" (I.199). His mother, too, nurtures "these growing thoughts" (I.227) by describing his auspicious, prophetic birth and parentage, including the humble as well as the glorious circumstances of his nativity (I.234-58). His awareness of discrepancy, like his mother's, is resolved by rightly and subjectively hearing identity in a hierarchy of the word rather than in establishmentarian logic alone.

> This having heard, strait I again revolv'd
> The Law and Prophets, searching what was writ
> Concerning the Messiah, to our Scribes
> Known partly, and soon found of whom they spake
> I am; this chiefly, that my way must lie
> Through many a hard assay ev'n to the death,
> E're I the promis'd Kingdom can attain,
> Or work Redemption for mankind, whose sins
> Full weight must be transferr'd upon my head.
>
> (I.259–67)

This identity, while it is cultic, perhaps echoing the divine "I am" of Yahweh to Moses (Exod. 3:14) as well as contextualizing the messianic prophecies,[3] does not distance the Son from the incipient congregation at the Jordan (and that of humankind hereafter) but rather joins him to them by suffering and by redemptive leadership. At first, then, the communion of saints expresses the mature state of mind nurtured by the Spirit and by the humble yet authorized ministry of Mary. Mary's nurturing here also anticipates the return to the mother's house at the close of the poem, where domesticity reflects Christianity's eventual return to the Spirit's nurture and a rebirth of the mystical body, the new kingdom. The mother's house will be an image of reformation as both return and departure in ministry, a focal point for the ongoing victory over Satan's secularized hierarchy in the world.[4]

John's initial reluctance to baptize one "much his greater," as the Son now remembers (I.278), if not overcome by the Son's humility, might have invited a regal and cultic identity for the Savior, a hierarchic reaction obviating the congregation's participatory experience of the mystical body. Instead, the Son's submissive attitude and John's sealing act sustain the community of believers by means of prophetic witness:

> I as all others to his Baptism came,
> Which I believ'd was from above; but he
> Strait knew me, and with loudest voice proclaim'd
> Me him (for it was shew'n him so from Heaven)
> Me him whose Harbinger he was; and first
> Refus'd on me his Baptism to confer.
>
> (I.273–78)

John's tending to structure their meeting according to a past hierarchy of messianic tradition is subdued by the Son's paradoxical insistence on a different kind of witness to authority. To this, John was "hardly won" (I.279), an early victory in terms of perception anticipating the Son's later victories over Satan's temptation to accept the wrong types of kingship. The Son's baptism by immersion ("But as I rose out of the laving stream" [I.280]) also signifies the relevance of his divinely mysterious immersion into humankind and mortality, and the importance of his bodily image to our concept of the church hereafter. "Th' Authority which I deriv'd from Heav'n" (I.289) will result in the Gospel's authority as rightly preached and as shared within the congregation of those baptized. Believers will participate in it because the Savior has shared in their washing and their mortality.[5] This divinely authorized gesture, both humble and inspiring, will in turn nurture the community of the faithful and remain a paradigm for the church. The ascent, like that of the Son's resurrected body, a new life out of the tomb, not only expresses divine authority but also enables future autobiographical witness to join mystically with the Gospel; his narrative, too, is a model for the testimony of "actual faith" of a sanctified member of the church.[6]

The tableau of John's baptism of the Son confirms a solidarity of relationship between man and God. His being led by the Spirit into the wilderness, however, is misinterpreted by Satan as apparent isolation. Satan's first disguise, "an aged man in Rural weeds" perhaps searching for "some stray Ewe" (I.314–15) echoes his desire to repeat his seduction of Eve with another victim, one separated from the protection of authority, he hopes, by pride, by the error of relegating authority to the self alone. Ironically, of course, his disguise reveals the sinister loneliness of a worldly, sometimes pathetic mind, one bent on drawing others into its desiccated understanding of life as death. He pretends curiosity and admiration of the Son's recognition by the prophet at the Jordan before entering "this place / So far from path or road of men," from whence a person alone never returns. Rather, "His Carcass, pin'd with hunger and with droughth" is likely to drop here (I.321–25). Even in this place, however, Satan continues, "Fame also finds us out" (I.334), and the "want" that sometimes constrains those dwelling in the wilderness to approach a village results in hearing the news (I.330–32).

The aged man seems a kind of shepherd, but one suggesting a reductive view of the congregation as well as of the Son who has come to redeem it.[7] Prophecy and witness in a community are for him merely fame and rumor. The inward and spatial certainty provided by the Spirit ("Who brought me hither" and who "Will bring me hence" [I.335–36]) is then recast problematically by the tempter: "By Miracle he may, reply'd the Swain, / What other way I see not" (I.337–38). The temptation to turn stones into bread, to "save thy self and us relieve / With Food" (I.344–45) would also reduce miraculous guidance or leadership to terms of secular ministry. The relationship between Christ and the community of believers would be conditioned by a material dependency, the body of the faithful defined economically. In reply, the Son asserts a hierarchy of the Word rather than of want, yet one subsuming contexts of hunger. He declares a prophetic heritage for the chosen of both the old and new covenants:

> Think'st thou such force in Bread? is it not written
> (For I discern thee other than thou seem'st)
> Man lives not by Bread only, but each Word

> Proceeding from the mouth of God; who fed
> Our Fathers here with Manna; in the Mount
> *Moses* was forty days, nor eat nor drank,
> And forty days *Elijah* without food
> Wander'd this barren waste, the same I now.

(I.347–54)

Moreover, Satan's demagogic appeal to fallen communities ironically occasions a rightly reasoned, affective sense of pastoral leadership in the Son. "Undisguis'd" Satan now announces himself as "that Spirit unfortunate, / Who leagu'd with millions more in rash revolt" fell from a "happy Station" (I.357–59). Nonetheless, he argues, he still participates in a fellowship somehow transcending boundaries of hell, heaven, and earth. He has "Large liberty" to associate "among the Sons of God" in heaven, at least "sometimes" (I.367–68), and can "love, at least contemplate and admire" one "Declar'd the Son of God" at the Jordan (I.380–85). He dwells "Copartner" in the world with mankind (I.392), giving direction for their future by "oracle, portents and dreams" (I.394–95). He is moved to join with mankind, he says, by obligation or debt, not by envy: "by them / I gain'd what I have gain'd" (I.390–91). His economy of partnership, however, overlooks the doctrinal worth of suffering as a means of communion, or, if he does appreciate the value of passionate atonement, he would undermine this significance for the Son:

> That fellowship in pain divides not smart,
> Nor lightens aught each mans peculiar load
> Small consolation then, were Man adjoyn'd:
> This wounds me most (what can it less) that Man,
> Man fall'n shall be restor'd, I never more.

(I.401–5)

Such quantitative rhetoric, of course, conveys to the Son that Satan's underlying appetite and motives are not really so balanced. The fear and perversity ("the pleasure to do ill" [I.422–23]) intuited by the Son as Satan's alienated psychology contrast tellingly with the fruitful suffering that will instead join man and God. Even an "Ejected, emptied, gaz'd, unpitied, shun'd" Satan (I.406), one to whom bliss is "no more communicable" (I.419), will inevitably serve "Heaven's King" (I.421), if only by rhetorical and psychological mischance.

Satan's perverse relationship with mankind has been absurdly mysti-

cal, his oracular religion founded on "more lies" (I.433) and reflecting the
identity of one "compos'd of lies" (I.407). But his resulting delusion of
glory and of power over nations worshipping at his shrines and temples
"shall be soon retrench'd" and "[he] no more with Pomp and Sacrifice /
Shalt be enquir'd at *Delphos* or elsewhere" (I.454–57), as the Son predicts.
Rather, true religion will be conveyed by a church whose teaching authority is
inwardly experienced by the congregation as God's will. Truth will then be
coterminous with the Spirit abiding in rightly reasoning minds and hearts:

> God hath now sent his living Oracle
> Into the World, to teach his final will,
> And sends his Spirit of Truth henceforth to dwell
> In pious Hearts, an inward Oracle
> To all truth requisite for man to know.
>
> (I.460–64)

The second book of the poem, however, begins with a crisis of belief
among "the new-baptiz'd" (II.1), the embryonic body of the faithful who
will receive the Spirit but who are now perplexed and doubting because of
the Son's material absence from the public eye. They too had heard "Jesus
Messiah Son of God declar'd" at the Jordan, "And on that high Authority
had believ'd" (II.4–5). Now their deliverance is complicated by an apparently vain search for him and by their lingering expectation of political as
well as prophetic salvation (II.13–48). Nevertheless, as if the Spirit were
already at work, or their own pious hearts preparing for the Spirit, they
begin to resolve the crisis by affective expression rather than by spatial
certainty. They expect Jesus to appear, but for them the Savior is already
figured affectively with the traits of pious hearts: "Soon we shall see our
hope, our joy return" (II.57). The visibly absent Son can yet breed faith and
hope in fellowship: "Thus they out of their plaints new hope resume / To
find whom at the first they found unsought" (II.58–59). Their sighs, like
the creek flowing into the sacred Jordan of the baptism, will be subsumed
by the wider play of the winds and of the divine Spirit:

> Then on the bank of *Jordan*, by a Creek
> Where winds with Reeds, and Osiers whisp'ring play
> Plain Fishermen, no greater men them call,
> Close in a Cottage low together got
> Thir unexpected loss and plaints out breath'd.
>
> (II.25–29)

Their loving complaint, too, uttered jointly, soon shifts into prayerful expressions of patience, even if their understanding of the Son's mission is still incomplete: "But let us wait; thus far he hath perform'd, / Sent his Annointed, and to us reveal'd him, / By his great Prophet" (II.49–51).

This more promising, transcendent irony, fostering patience after the Son's disappearance, is also personified in Mary's "troubl'd thoughts, which she in sighs thus clad" (II.65). She is already accustomed to patience in mood and as a virtue (II.102), and memories of young Jesus seemingly lost in the Temple enhance the mystery of "his absence now," an intentional obscurity for "some great purpose" (II.100–101). Her thoughts are "Meekly compos'd," and she awaits "the fulfilling" as she has "Since [she] first her Salutation heard" (II.107–8). The generative, fruitful outcome of patience in belief is associated in her mind with conceiving her Son in her encounter with the Holy Spirit. Humility still binds her to God and Messiah, and paradoxes of honor without circumstantial glory in her personal testament complement the prophetic witness shared by the developing community of the faithful:

> O what avails me now that honour high
> To have conceiv'd of God, or that salute,
> Hail highly favour'd, among women blest;
> While I to sorrows am no less advanc't,
> And fears as eminent, above the lot
> Of other women, by the birth I bore,
> In such a season born when scarce a Shed
> Could be obtain'd to shelter him or me
> From the bleak air; a Stable was our warmth.
>
> (II.66–74)

The "bleak air" and her fears are suffused with a humility understood as divinely significant, and her recollection, "a Stable was our warmth," does not sound bitter or resentful. Her patient conclusion, "Afflicted I may be, it seems, and blest; / I will not argue that, nor will repine" (II.93–94), prevents the selfish autobiographical logic such as Satan (and once Eve) pursues, and subordinates both rhetoric and desire to prophetic statements of God's will she has heard and felt, if not yet pondered discursively. Her "heart hath been a store-house long of things / And sayings laid up, portending strange events," she adds (II.103–4), implying how the wealth and nourishment of the word is guarded in an affective domain until God's time for promulgating the news. Her question and answer, "But where delays he now? some great intent / Conceals him" (II.95–96), as had occurred in the Temple years before, now locates the Son as a viable memory having a present, edifying meaning. His material place seems less important than one's inward experience of him:

> I lost him, but so found, as well I saw
> He could not lose himself; but went about
> His Father's business; what he meant I mus'd,
> Since understand; much more his absence now
> Thus long to some great purpose he obscures.
>
> (II.97–101)

Mary also remembers Herod's bloodthirsty reaction to the uncertain whereabouts of the infant Jesus ("the Murd'rous King / . . . who sought his life, and missing fill'd / With Infant blood the streets of *Bethlehem*" [II.76–78]), the violent tendency of secular kingship and of the egocentric mind attempting, as Satan does, to reduce prophecy to the self's domain. Rather, the "Private, unactive, calm, contemplative" life of Jesus in Nazareth, a life "Little suspicious t' any King" (II.81–82), better establishes the identity of a divine Lord whose presence can be everywhere felt. This Christological identity has been "own'd from Heav'n by his Father's voice" and at the same time acknowledged in public by John (II.83–85). Even though "some great change" (II.86) to visible honor does not occur, a prophetic context of meaning has been generated that encompasses all the humiliating, political events. As a sign of fulfillment, maturing, and communion, the baptismal event again anticipates a church body challenged by worldly suspicion, yet encouraging the heart pierced by the pain of loss during the Son's work, his Father's business. While her mood is also one of affliction, Mary implicitly exalts the simultaneous presence of the mystical body in heaven, on earth, and in the mind. Unlike Satan's and Herod's reductions of truth to the realm of a merely pathetic destiny, Mary's meditation welcomes divine possibility.

The Son's concurrent introspection is also a generative and opening mood rather than a reductive one. His meditation complements his mother's brooding and prophetic memory; her fruitful waiting for the divine significance of events to unfold ("with thoughts / Meekly compos'd awaited the fulfilling" [II.108]) resonates now with the solemn message given to her at the Annunciation and with her memories of the Nativity. The Son's brooding is cooperative with hers and therefore with the solemn message, if it is also a structuring of events more actively for the world hereafter in a way characteristic of male heroism and its mythic prerogatives:

> The while her Son tracing the Desert wild,
> Sole but with holiest Meditations fed
> Into himself descended, and at once
> All his great work to come before him set;
> How to begin, how to accomplish best
> His end of being on Earth, and mission high.
>
> (II.109–14)

His mission will not be ecclesiastic in the establishmentarian sense, but his "great work," like Mary's understanding and nurture, will sustain a body of the faithful in which affliction and patience can also be exaltation.[8]

Satan's body of followers, on the other hand, seems both enclosed and arrogant—"Each his own reign allotted" over the elements of fire, water, earth and air (II.123). His invisible agents serve an egoistic pastorate of self-aggrandizing sophistry and aestheticism; his "Spirits likest to himself in guile," "at hand," in order "to unfold some active Scene" (II.237–39) compensate for his fears while exercising an outmoded, illusory authority over creative energy. The courtly scene or masque then produced is similarly outmoded, transparent in its mechanisms and tastelessness when viewed by an aesthetically enlightened shepherd.

The poem's contrasting pastoral motives also allude to a reformed perception of the eucharistic banquet, the congregational seal complementing baptism. The Son is looking for "Sheep-cote or Herd" (II.287) to end his fast and, presumably, to associate with common shepherds. He finds Satan's ornate, artificial pastoral scenes in a cathedral-like forest of error, where beauty is shadowed with flattery and where courtly style defends a threatened monarchy of wit:

> High rooft and walks beneath, and alleys brown
> That open'd in the midst a woody Scene,
> Natures own work it seem'd (Nature taught Art)
> And to a Superstitious eye the haunt
> Of Wood-Gods and Wood-Nymphs; he view'd it round
> When suddenly a man before him stood,
> Not rustic as before, but seemlier clad,
> As one in City, or Court, or Palace bred.
>
> (II.293–300)

On one level, the shade, brown alleys, high roof, the appeal to superstition, and the courtly costume are a sylvan cathedral—an inauthentic temple spoiling nature and art with the kind of mystery that is merely hierarchic obscurantism. Such visual egoism might overshadow true religion by spectacle and "fair speech" (II.301). Additionally, the magic banquet, "In ample space under the broadest shade / A Table richly spred, in regal mode" (II.339–40), suggests the unholy alliance between courtly decadence and a wrongheaded eucharistic discipline.[9]

Rightly understood and practiced in "true religion," the Lord's Supper is analogous to baptism. Both sacraments are not liturgically necessary for many reformers, Milton included, although they are the only sacraments recognized as such in the church discipline Milton apparently follows. Rather, many have been saved without them, or received the gifts of the Spirit by the word and faith. Essentially, the Eucharist is doctrine and not a sanctifying operation in itself. Its efficacy is figurative or metaphorical, a spiritual bread, not Christ's mortal or transubstantiated flesh. Like baptism, the Eucharist commemorates and seals the benefits of Christ's death for believers. Implicitly, the eucharistic banquet, like baptism, signifies and reinforces the mystical body of the faithful. *De Doctrina* cites 1 Corinthians: "The bread which we break, is it not the communion of the body of Christ? Since the bread is one, we many are one body, for we all partake of that one bread." The sacrament as doctrine declares the faith linking the believer to Christ:

> That living bread which, Christ says, is his flesh, and the true drink which, he says, is his blood, can only be the doctrine which teaches us that Christ was made man in order to pour out his blood for us. The man who accepts this doctrine with true faith will live forever. This is as certain as that actual eating and drinking sustain this mortal life of ours for a little while, indeed, much more certain. For it means that Christ will dwell in us and we in him. . . . (Yale Prose, 6:553–54)

In the poem, Satan's repeated invitation to the Son "to sit and eat" and not to suspect this food has any connection with "Fruits forbidd'n" or "knowledge, . . . at least of evil" (*P.R.,* II.369–71) is also an attempt to disrupt the doctrinal message of the Son's very human hunger and thirst. The Son's rejoinder to Satan, "And with my hunger what hast thou to do?" (II.389), reveals that his hunger derives from divine as well as human choice. It is not an involuntary participation in the fallen heritage of humankind, doomed because of appetite and always drawn to spectacles of appetite.

The Son's "right" and "pow'r" (II.379–80) are yet authoritative, and he anticipates the solemn banquet near the end of the poem:

> I can at will, doubt not, as soon as thou,
> Command a Table in this Wilderness,
> And call swift flights of Angels ministrant
> Array'd in Glory on my cup t' attend.
>
> (II.383–86)

The banquet fit for the true king, the Christ, would better signify his divinity as well as his humanity, angels ministering to and celebrating the condition he has heroically chosen of hunger and mortality. Satan's meretricious feast, on the other hand, obscures the prospect of doctrine with a passive experience of sensuous indulgence while it insinuates demonic and statist authority. It is the kind of banquet that might enervate a hero rather than nurture him, and its "pompous Delicacies" (II.390) result in unmasking the ironically servile role of the giver.

The angelic banquet after Satan's fall, on the other hand, is not burdened with culinary and courtly artifacts. It is broadly described as food from both heaven's and earth's garden in order to indicate both natures in the Son:

> A table of Celestial Food, Divine,
> Ambrosial, Fruits fetcht from the tree of life,
> And from the fount of life Ambrosial drink,
> That soon refresh'd him wearied, and repair'd
> What hunger, if aught hunger, had impair'd.
>
> (IV.588–92)

Verbal elaboration in this legitimately mystical banquet is not only a heavenly pastoral and courtesy but also a lyric celebration of doctrine, a new psalmody or "Heavenly Anthems of his victory" (IV.594) who, as "heir of both worlds," is about to begin the "glorious work" of atonement (IV.633–35). The angels then sing Satan's ultimate defeat and terror (IV.625–29), but also rehearse a heritage of affective authority in worship that can nurture "more surely" than sacramental bread:

> Thus they the Son of God our Saviour meek
> Sung Victor, and from Heav'nly Feast refresht
> Brought on his way with joy.
>
> (IV.636–38)

Satan had just challenged the Son by means of didactic authority, applying what is "written" (IV.556) to a leap of faith construed categorically, his prophetic text framed by a need for rhetorical and discursive conviction rather than for spiritual sustenance:

> I to thy Fathers house
> Have brought thee, and highest plac't, highest is best,
> Now shew thy Progeny; if not to stand,
> Cast thy self down; safely if Son of God:
> For it is written, He will give command
> Concerning thee to his Angels, in thir hands
> They shall up lift thee. . . .
>
> (IV.552–58)

The Son's climactic reply, citing Moses' commentary on the first commandment (Deut. 6:16), demonstrates the doctrine of right worship as his sustaining strength against doubt and despair: "also it is written, / Tempt not the Lord thy God, he said and stood" (IV.560–61). In this context, the statement and image may not be intended as a declaration of divine identity itself as simply peremptory, although it certainly refers us to other contexts in the poem where divine identity is appreciated by Mary and by the Son from past evidence (I.233ff.; II.67ff.). Rather, his citation and standing show figuratively and iconically that heroic identity means the solemn assimilation of doctrine, here to the extent that the Father's doctrinal intent is coterminous with the Son's state of mind and crucial position in history. So nourished, he is one witnessing against the mystical body's adversary— the Tempter once standing with him on the verge of the New Testament but who now falls "smitten with amazement" (IV.562), having heard clear doctrine preached in a voice unimpeded by worldliness or fear.[10]

The paradigmatic ecclesiology of the hero's arriving at a point ensuring the adversary's defeat by means of prophetic witness to Scripture and by standing while witnessing God's truth (an implicit figure of sanctification, if not of divinity) summarizes his lesser victories over problematic hierarchies.[11] In book II, for example, Satan had also argued that authority depends on satisfying the appetitive cravings of the multitude, on means that Jesus conspicuously lacks:

> thy self
> Bred up in poverty and streights at home;
> Lost in a Desert here and hunger-bit:

> Which way or from what hope dost thou aspire
> To greatness? whence Authority deriv'st
> What Followers, what Retinue canst thou gain,
> Or at thy heels the dizzy Multitude,
> Longer then thou canst feed them on thy cost?
>
> (II.414–21)

Jesus replies that he rejects both "Riches and Realms" (II.458) for the internal kingdom of a virtuous self, that which in turn can "guide Nations in the way of truth / By saving Doctrine" (II.474). This virtuous knowledge leads nations from error,

> and from errour lead
> To know, and knowing worship God aright,
> Is yet more Kingly, this attracts the Soul,
> Governs the inner man, the nobler part,
> That other o're the body only reigns,
> And oft by force, which to a generous mind
> So reigning can be no sincere delight.
>
> (II.474–80)

The "generous mind" is a psychology anticipating right worship; worshiping God "aright" expresses a kingly self-esteem, a selfhood that "attracts" as well as "governs." In this way, too, a national body is better led. The structures associated with internal worship and its ethical administration of the "inner man" are better guides than the external application of hierarchies that may be insincere or tyrannically forceful. A priori, self-discipline should generate, not merely reflect, ecclesiastical and political systems.

In book III, Satan attempts to confuse this issue by concretizing it as an opportunity to redeem and to lead "by conquest or by league" the dispersed tribes of Israel (III.370ff.). In rejecting the offer, Jesus again emphasizes the impropriety of "*Israel's* true King" (III.441) heading captive tribes not worshiping aright, those who "wrought their own captivity" by idolatry and by the extremes of appetite, "thir other worse than heathenish crimes" (III.414–19). Those who are still "Unhumbl'd, unrepentant, unreform'd" (III.429) in worship as well as in ethics are not ready for the Son's kind of leadership. Rather, they have prevented a renovative communion among themselves and with the Lord, choosing error as policy in order to preserve mistaken pride, and leaving "a race behind / Like to themselves" distinguishable only by "Circumcision vain" (III.423–25), i.e., by a ritual no longer expressing or sealing right worship and covenant. Instead, circumcision, for reformers a type of baptism in the old law, here signifies a compulsion to perpetuate error and vanity, and so to preserve the ego as its own place by means of cultism.[12] One underlying appeal of this temptation, of course, is its sensuously aesthetic elaboration of military and political display, the "ostentation vain of fleshly arm, / And fragile arms" (III.387–88), a dramatic tableau that again projects Satan's yearning for dominion over creation's realm and over the divine scheme. Jesus then rightly concludes that God's "due time and providence" (III.440), not the agenda of a worldly king, dictate a return to the Promised Land. Meanwhile, "let them serve / Thir enemies, who serve Idols with God" (III.430–31)—a conditional statement that describes Satan's actual role as well as that of the dispersed tribes.

Although the time of returning to the Promised Land is known only to God (and the compromised situation of the ten tribes makes an immediate return unlikely), the tone of the Son's speech implies his longing for their reunion, and not a self-righteous pleasure in their excommunication:

> Yet he at length, time to himself best known,
> Remembring *Abraham* by some wond'rous call
> May bring them back repentant and sincere,
> And at their passing cleave th' *Assyrian* flood,
> While to their native land with joy they hast,
> As the Red Sea and *Jordan* once he cleft,
> When to the promis'd land thir Fathers pass'd.
>
>   (III.433–39)

The distance caused by their error and vanity is nearly overcome by his ministerial state of mind, a mood both authoritative and nurturing. "Due time and providence" in this context also suggests the possibility of spiritual rebirth—a return to the land of birth and religious nurture "with joy" and with sincere repentance rather than with merely cultic conformity or opportunism. The Son subordinates his will to the Father's in regarding the return, but his paradigmatic identity as the authorized pastor is demonstrated as well. He seizes the occasion in the sense of anticipating his pastoral, affective role as head of the mystical body.[13]

When the Son disdains all the kingdoms Satan imagines are in his power to offer him, he instead emphasizes the unlimited realm of his redeemed kingdom (IV.151). The intellectual and aesthetic kingdom Satan then promises— "so let extend thy mind o're all the world" (IV.223)—is also rejected as "vain boast / Or subtle shifts conviction to evade" when exhibited by proud Stoics (IV.307–8). The prophesied kingdom, too, including the prophecy of "Violence and stripes, and lastly cruel death" (IV.388), is a rhetorical weapon for Satan, but one again turned into victory for the Son by means of an affective hermeneutic. In Satan's troubled, ironic musing, the stars have prophesied a kingdom of some temporal kind, one limited by boundary or by categorical logic:

> A Kingdom they portend thee, but what Kingdom,
> Real or Allegoric I discern not,
> Nor when, eternal sure, as without end,
> Without beginning; for no date prefixt
> Directs me in the Starry Rubric set.
>
> (IV.389–93)

Now desperately seeking to resolve the paradox, and thereby shape prophecy to his will, Satan simultaneously invades the realms of heaven, earth, and the mind by storm. The storm here (IV.394–431), like the shipwreck of *Lycidas*, cannot permanently disable a mystical pastorate, its fury succeeded by an inexorable light of day. Rather, it tellingly magnifies the state of Satan's predicament and, too, the Adamic heritage of unreasoning fear always lurking in alienated creation. If "Not yet expir'd" (IV.395), Satan's power over matter and mind is ultimately derivative and reactive, serving the Creator's authority and reinforcing the portable hell of his excommunication from the mystical body by the irony of his temporary manipulation of the world's body. His insidious interpretation of the storm's significance first recalls Adam's didactic consolation of Eve after her nightmare ("Evil into the mind of God or Man / May come and go, so unapprov'd, and leave / No spot or blame behind" [*P.L.*, V.117–19]), but soon attempts to revive the prospect of fear. "These flaws, though mortals fear them," Satan explains,

> Are to the main as inconsiderable,
> And harmless, if not wholsom, as a sneeze
> To mans less universe, and soon are gone;
> Yet as being oft times noxious where they light
> On man, beast, plant, wastful and turbulent,
> Like turbulencies in th' affairs of men,
> Over whose heads they roar, and seem to point,
> They oft fore-signifie and threaten ill.
>
> (IV.453–64)

Such advice regarding the consequences of rejecting "The perfet season" for kingly ambition (IV.468) in Israel is transparent to the Son, who rightly refers it to his adversary's ambition and stormy frustration (IV.495–96). The water and fire that are by Satan "In ruin reconcil'd" (IV.413) instead signify the Son's reconciliation of the ruined, Adam and Eve's issue, and his own contemplative bearing as he emerges from the storm and dreams: "Mee worse than wet thou find'st not; other harm / Those terrors which thou speak'st of, did me none" (IV.486–77). In time, his sacrificial reconciling of identities, like his simultaneously cosmic ("Real") and contemplative ("Allegoric") kingdoms, will abide as saving doctrine. Now "walking on a Sunny hill" (IV.447), where we can presume he again meditates his ministry to come, the Son dismisses Satan's baptismal travesty of water, fire, wind, and fear as the key to mysterious identity and indirectly compels Satan to return to the truth revealed at the Jordan. Satan argues he had applied to the baptized Jesus, "call'd / The Son of God" (IV.516–18), the "narrower Scrutiny" (IV.515) in order to understand and somehow exploit the revelation of identity. All along it has been a denial of ineluctable knowledge, of course, a hollow, ironic tyranny over mind and world driving Satan to the Temple's height where doctrine is witnessed rather than reduced or impeded by fear and egoism.

As a mystical body, the church, like the Son standing over the Temple and preaching the Father's word, stands away from worldliness, although the world's kingdoms and ministers are always near at hand, waiting to assault it. As a cultural entity, the church may necessarily return to the wilderness because of kings; but there it draws its members together, preparing them for God's call while they are "in a hidden state," as Milton's contemporary, Henry Vane, put it in *The Face of the Times* (1662).[14] In *Paradise Regain'd*, however, the time for the Son's work is gloriously now, as the angels sing: "Queller of Satan, on thy glorious work / Now enter, and begin to save mankind" (IV.634–35). Paradoxically, at the end of the poem this trumpet call fades into a quietly domestic note:

> Thus they the Son of God our Saviour meek
> Sung Victor, and from Heav'nly Feast refresht
> Brought on his way with joy; hee unobserv'd
> Home to his Mothers house private return'd.

> (IV.636–39)

The internalized mood of joy and the nourishment of the heavenly feast provided by the Father's kingdom may here be regarded as also a maternal influence, an affective and private (or silent) experience of doctrine. The mother's house, too, is a kind of *ecclesia* nurturing the body of the church.[15] The humble yet exalted interior of the childhood home, like that of Mary's womb, or the stable of the Nativity, or eventually, earth's house, the Easter tomb, will bring forth the good news of saving doctrine. Jesus will preach in the Temple, as he did when a boy on his Father's business, and preach to hungry multitudes outside the holy city in the Gospel narratives. Milton, however, also directs our attention to the ecclesiastic heritage of the Son's victory as first a return to simple but authoritative discipline.

5

True Religion
and Tragedy

In the early twentieth century, an "old" historicism derived from the Cambridge school of anthropology sought to uncover layers of "prerational" meaning in ancient Greek drama, especially in the plays' reflections of the myths and rituals of primitive folk religion.[1] Criticism of Renaissance biblical drama had been reluctant to follow suit until the current generation of postmodernists and "new" historicists began to emphasize the "prerational" impulses and patriarchal tyrannies possibly underlying the aesthetic constructions of any religious discourse, whether orthodox or pagan. In the old historicism, the prevailing critical view had been that the dubious rationality and the undeniable violence of many biblical narratives had ultimate cultural meanings that were missing from classical myth, and that imitations of Greek drama using biblical characters were inspired by a higher logic than that of ancient Dionysian celebration. If an aura of obscure ritual remained in these imitations—i.e., when a biblical hero was divinely motivated or tragically sacrificed—it was subsumed by a typological consciousness shared by author and reader, which saw the wisdom of God's providential design for salvation beyond the catastrophe. Sometimes an explicit typological allusion was added to the plot if the Old Testament story did not seem to make the eventual outcome quite clear enough. Milton's contemporary, Hugo Grotius, for instance, had the hero of his Old Testament tragedy *Iosephus* prophesy about the future Redeemer who, like Joseph, would sojourn in Egypt, and Joos van den Vondel subtitled his 1660 dramatic version of the Samson story "Holy Revenge."[2]

Milton's biblical tragedy, the "dramatic poem" *Samson Agonistes* (1671), has a more celebrated history than these forgotten works, of course, but what is now seen as the controversial nature of its unrelieved Hebraism has become a central issue for interpreters. Although written by a famous polemicist for the radical Christianity of his time, *Samson Agonistes* has no Messianic prophecy or pronounced typological vision of Christian redemption, no moment when its tragic hero glimpses the course of salvation history as Milton's Adam does in *Paradise Lost*. To be sure, a biblical tragedy is not a biblical epic, and the traditional epic convention of prophetic scenes such as we find in *Paradise Lost* may have been beyond the scope and literary decorum of tragedy as Milton construed the genre. Nonetheless, the biblical Samson is somehow an important figure in the culture of a Christian poet, and writing a tragedy about him—rather than an epic—has not, apparently, settled the question of his religious significance for modern readers.

The current critical debate on the issue of typological significance often returns to the ritual, or sacrificial, meaning of Samson's tragic, if also heroic, death. The affirmative declares that *Samson Agonistes* does have a visionary perspective, that Samson's final act in Dagon's temple is both tragic and good, a redemptive act consistent with biblical types of Christian sacrifice. Thomas Stroup, for example, finds stages of regeneration in Milton's text that imitate ceremonial structures in the *Book of Common Prayer,* and he states that the work is eventually sacramental or eucharistic because Samson "has offered himself for his people and has kept his covenant through his ritual."[3] Sherman Hawkins also concludes that Samson is a true sacrifice, "offering himself in the likeness of one who is both priest and victim" and contradicting the falsely eucharistic feast of Dagon.[4] Michael Lieb, while not suggesting a specific sacramental analogue, interprets Samson's renewed Nazaritic cultism as consistent with a "true sacrificium" and his "rouzing motions" as coterminous with the divine impulse Milton mentions in *De Doctrina*, an aspect of the same Holy Spirit that anointed Jesus.[5] In the broad sense of the term, such readings of *Samson* may be described as "liturgical" in that they refer to forms of worship in attempting to explain Samson's heroism. Here, the emphasis on allusions to Christian worship in the work is continuous with the thesis of an eventually regenerate Samson, a position perhaps best represented by Mary Ann Radzinowicz, who regards Samson's recovery as inspiring and his deed against the Philistines and their temple a "beneficit action" that restores hope and creativity.[6]

Perhaps the most forceful dissenter from redemptive readings of *Samson Agonistes*, and a critic who implicitly departs from seeing edifying sacrifice as thematically or structurally significant in the work, is Joseph Wittreich.

There is no Christian typology in *Samson Agonistes*, Wittreich believes, except what may be construed ironically by the reader. The poem is not a celebration of inspired religious heroism. Milton's Samson is not a deliverer, and those characters in the text who think he is are deluded. Rather, he is a vengeful, distracted, unethical failure, and his psychology is comparable to that which was "objectified and legalized in those religions of cruelty" characteristic of the seventeenth century. To Wittreich, an attentive reader would regard *Samson* as a pessimistic dramatic work in contrast to *Paradise Regain'd*, the epic of the true Savior, which precedes it in Milton's 1671 volume.[7]

Not all interpretations of the work's religious significance are so diametrically opposed. Among a middle-of-the-road group, Ernest B. Gilman and Joan S. Bennet find traits of redemptive sacrifice in Milton's characterization of Samson and at the same time a stultifying establishmentarianism among the Danites. Samson changes for the better, Bennet argues, but the Chorus does not. Like the prelates of seventeenth-century Anglicanism, they remain bound by the mentality of "carnal" legalism. They are "pious followers of the Lord, but incapable of faith." Samson, however, eventually "reaches the limits of the old law and hence is able to transcend and fulfill it."[8] He therefore reflects Milton's adherence to the cause of Christian liberty. Gilman also positions himself on the side of renovation in *Samson*; but, he concludes, the tragedy as "play" is intended to frustrate audience expectation, just as Samson's theatrical performance frustrates the expectations of the Philistines. The reader's response is thereby shifted from an appreciation of spectacle to an internal vision, from various idolatries to a better and reformist sense of the word. Samson's blindness is compensated by a spiritual insight the Philistines lack; he has a "superior inner vision" that enables him to end his life "heroically at noon." Nonetheless, Gilman continues, disconcerting remnants of external spectacle linger in the prevailing culture of the Danites. Viewed from the reader's perspective, Manoa's proposed monument to Samson "will be a stony thing that only petrifies the outward features of Samson's 'adventures.'"[9] Bennet and Gilman seem to represent the current trend, one that questions the "alleged 'regeneration' of Samson," as Ashraf Rushdy puts it, but without discarding the thesis of a divinely sanctioned catastrophe.[10]

My own position generally accords with this recent trend. I see Milton's Samson as neither a vengeful monster nor an unqualified success as a religious and national hero. At the same time, however, I wish to argue that ecclesiastic and liturgical allusions in the text are central to an understanding of

Milton's views of Samson as a tragic rather than epic hero. Samson's tragic identity, I hope to show, derives from Milton's association of "true religion" (i.e., a faith free from prescriptive ritual) with the epic domain of reformed Christians: the domain of Adam in *Paradise Lost*, who perceives the necessity of a Reformation, and of the Son in *Paradise Regain'd*, who engenders the paradigm of the church as a mystical body of believers. The ecclesiastical heritage prevailing in *Samson*, but not in Milton's epic contexts, shows the unhappy impediments to true religion fostered by a hero who loses sight of the beginning and the end of history, even though he grasps and destroys the evil of the moment.

To argue this case, I first compare liturgical allusions in Milton's epics to those of *Samson Agonistes*. Following this, I explore the way Samson's tragic insight is clouded by establishmentarian religiosity when he proudly rejects the temptations of Dalila and Harapha to relax his guard as husband and as defender of the faith. Finally, I discuss how the dialogue between Manoa and the Messenger about Samson's death unconsciously sustains the problematic, cultic heritage of mediated truth.

By placing *Paradise Regain'd* before *Samson Agonistes*, Milton encourages us to see the contrast between the epic hero and a political champion whose motives are otherwise sanctionable. The Gospel temptations of Jesus, *Paradise Regain'd*'s biblical source, have an acceptable formulaic function, but as part of the liturgy of the word, which for reformers is a necessary and sufficient set of prescriptions prior to and perhaps more important than sacrificial ritual in a Christian service. The Gospel, like the Son, stands unaffected by Satan or by the dim egoism and ornament of prelatical discipline. Samson, however, if he at first gropes darkly for the guiding hand of a true and disestablished context for faith, eventually seizes the opportunity for national rather than mystical identity—for a magnified but enclosed vehicle for fame like that of the monumental tomb promised by his father to the Chorus. Manoa, Dalila, and Harapha, along with the Danites, serve to reflect Samson's grand, closed perspective of the past. Samson's pride is an ironically sterile kind of nationalism underlying both his derelict and finally aroused moods. It is this flaw which precludes the transforming of Samson's personal witness to error from tragic to epic and which allows him to provide a timely rescue of the oppressed but not a typology of timeless atonement. He would preserve the political and cultural body of the Danites as a reflection of his reviving physical and cultic dignity, but his sacrifice obscures a more fruitful heritage of Adam and Eve: that of doctrinal certainty about the commonality of sin. Although Samson's limited independence from a patriarchy that has declined into establishmentarianism and his righteous iconoclasm imply the reform of church discipline claimed by the Independents and Separatists of Milton's time, Samson's inability to conceive a body of saving doctrine free from mythographic enclosures parallels the recurrent failure of reformist as well as prelatical leadership to apply tragic knowledge fruitfully, to shift the focus of believers from the political body to the mystical body.

In *Of True Religion* (1673), Milton defines the term in the commonly Protestant way: "True Religion is the true Worship and Service of God, learnt and believed from the Word of God only." "False Religion," especially Catholicism, "is a Religion taken up and believ'd from the traditions of men, and additions to the word of God" (Yale Prose, 8:419, 421). The present danger to faith may be lessened in four ways: (1) by an intolerance of Catholic practice ("first we must remove their idolatry, and all the furniture thereof"); (2) by an intramural tolerance of debate among Protestants themselves (by laying "contraries" together, whereby, as in logic, "falsehood will appear more false, and truth the more true"); (3) by regular Bible reading; and (4) by sincere repentance in the lives of the English people (Yale Prose, 8:431, 438–39).

Milton's Samson is both repentant and mindful of scripture. Moreover, his destruction of the Dagon idol would be interpreted by many of Milton's readers as righteously consistent with anti-Catholic iconoclasm. (The *Oxford English Dictionary* cites a specifically anti-Catholic usage of "Dagon" in 1677.) He is also willing to risk (or perhaps indulge) extending his heroic identity beyond unnecessary legalisms. The cultural figuration or commemorative ritual of his sacrifice, however, is later authorized by temporal occasions and by patriarchy, not by the ageless text of the Gospel, just as his death itself is "by accident" in the words Milton uses summarizing the action in the Argument. He cannot elude the edifice of religion, the accidental theater in which faith's prophetic form—the tragic knowledge of the hero—is obscured by histrionic vanity. Drawn to a vicarious empowerment, Manoa and the Danites will celebrate an imaginary figure, a Samson "Like *Samson*" (*S.A.,* line 1710), and denigrate the significance of the derelict captive, who is a microcosmic figure of the world's sinful body. Samson's righteous iconoclasm, Milton's readers would know from the original narrative in Judges, was affected by motives of personal revenge unheard by the Messenger in the dramatic poem—a discrepancy perhaps guiding readers back to the biblical text for a more authoritative moral guidance than is provided by aesthetic celebrations of that text or of the event. Characteristically, the choral celebration of the event in the poem, the analogue of a Hebraic ritual that will incorporate Samson, aesthetically figures his secret, explosively declared power (lines 1597ff.) rather than the mutuality of sin as the cause of so much death. The mythic creature that "reflourishes" is still "fame," "A secular bird of ages" (lines 1704–7), and Samson's sacrifice will accordingly be subjected to ulterior contexts and ceremonies of mythographic and hierarchic intent.

If we compare the ecclesiological allusions in Milton's epics to those in *Samson*, we can see that the degree of heroic independence and self-knowledge needed to foster true religion is better depicted in the Son's rejection of fame, a stance so rare as to amaze the Son's tempter in *Paradise Regain'd*. The epic hero in a context suggesting the ecclesiology of true religion is like the generically different or independent nature of Miltonic epic itself; he subsumes tragedy and is himself a truly comprehensive figure. The Gospel characterizations of the epics issue from a poet (who ought to be "a true poem") pursuing "Things unattempted yet in Prose or Rime." The historical course of religion, like that of merely conventional aesthetic practice, has been rather the opposite: it has reflected a recurring secularization of form, as we are reminded by Michael's prophecy in *Paradise Lost* and by Milton's preface to *Samson Agonistes*. But, happily, Milton's epic narratives eventually present a comedic sense of history: "Ages of endless date / Founded in righteousness and peace and love, / To bring forth fruits Joy and eternal Bliss" (*P.L.,* XII.549–51). In *Paradise Regain'd*, "A fairer Paradise is founded now / For *Adam* and his chosen Sons" (*P.R.,* IV.613–14), a place subsuming tragic history yet also a consciousness informed by tragic knowledge. Religion, however, obscures rather than clarifies the significance of tragic history for the "farr greater part." The "living Temples" of personhood, informed by tragic knowledge and thereby rightly suited for enshrining faith and conscience, will have their moral psychology vandalized by "Secular power" masquerading as "Spiritual Laws" (*P.L.,* XII.517–32). So Michael tells Adam:

Whence heavie persecution shall arise
On all who in the worship persevere
Of Spirit and Truth; the rest, farr greater part,
Will deem in outward Rites and specious formes
Religion satisfi'd: Truth shall retire
Bestuck with slandrous darts, and works of Faith
Rarely be found; so shall the World goe on,
To good malignant, to bad men benigne,
Under her own waight groaning, till the day
Appeer of respiration to the just,
And vengeance to the wicked, at return
Of him so lately promis'd to thy aid.

(XII.530–42)

The historical counterparts of those persevering in true religion are the "Unsung" heroes, who are implicitly more substantial or real than mythographic figures. They are the faithful who are declared "Heroic" by the epic singer in the invocation to book IX of *Paradise Lost* when he "now must change / Those Notes" of "discourse unblam'd" to "Tragic" (lines 5–6). Both in the episode of original sin, "breach / Disloyal on the part of Man" (lines 6–7), and, later, after the fall, in a scene showing Adam and Eve penitent, worshiping in a tragically informed way (XI.1099), the poetic figures characteristic of chivalric Romance would be an indecorous distraction. Rather, this tragic context (eventually a marital typology and choreography of the reformed body of Christianity) belittles the gestures of "gorgious Knights" and "tinsel Trappings," the aesthetics "of Artifice or Office mean" (IX.36–39) that decorate conventional heroic narratives but do not actually inform them. Contemporary, staged tragedy, as Milton complains in the preface to *Samson Agonistes*, is similarly misinformed or unreformed, "absurd," mixing inessential ("Comic stuff") with substance in order "corruptly to gratifie the people"; i.e., it is formulated for temporal gain, for a secular dominion over the people rather than serving as liturgical analogues—as works for and of the people, as the etymology of "liturgy" suggests.

In *Samson Agonistes*, the heritage of sin as the premise of a rightly informed culture is similarly implied but then obscured by celebrations of heroic fame, and by the degeneration of heroic love into tribal possessiveness. The hero, Samson, enters the world of the dramatic poem as a blind protagonist asking to be guided onward, even "A little onward" in the opening line. But, here, the role of the guide is textually ambiguous; he is a presence that may or may not be felt by the hero (or imagined by the reader); the guide is speechless.

Samson at first regards himself as psychologically imprisoned by his unheroic predicament. He is breathing easier because of what "Superstition yields" on Dagon's festival day, a time prohibiting "Laborious works." However, "Retiring from the popular noise," he finds "Ease to the body some, none to the mind / From restless thoughts" (*S.A.,* lines 14–18). In his alienated, self-centered mood, his stinging memories—of what he was compared to what he is—are not creatively relegated by him to a community of belief. As Bennet has observed, "There is no channel in the Mosaic law by which what virtue he has . . . can compensate for his wrongs."[11] He can feel "The breath of Heav'n fresh- blowing, pure and sweet," but the sensation does not suggest any spiritual relief (*S.A.,* lines 6–19). His breaking "the Seal of silence" required of Nazarites resulted in his blindness and disgrace, and he sees himself excluded from God's "prime decree":

> O first created Beam, and thou great Word,
> Let there be light, and light was over all;
> Why am I thus bereav'd thy prime decree?
> The Sun to me is dark
> And silent as the Moon,
> When she deserts the night
> Hid in her vacant interlunar cave.

(lines 83–89)

The creational image is partly a memory of Genesis, a primary epic, and this significant narrative of origins, sin, and reconciliation may answer Samson's question more completely than his personal history. Yet he will not be reconciled to epic time. His hammering lament, "O dark, dark, dark, amid the blaze of noon" (line 80), situates his guilty mood and "evil Conscience"—to borrow the term from *Paradise Lost* (X.849), where Adam appears similarly absolute in hopelessness—in tragic time, the point of the fall. Adam, fortunately, experiences the grace and nurture of forgiveness, his later mood conditioned by Eve's supplicating love and by Michael's enlightening, prophetic ministry. Samson might forgive Dalila's sin, but he will not be reconciled to her as heathenish wife; his "pardon" of her is actually self-centered: "Such pardon as I give my folly, / Take to thy wicked deed" (*S.A.,* lines 825–26).

Samson's recovering self-esteem and cultic identity, and their iconoclastic expression, do not seem spiritually fruitful in Milton's treatment.

His motions and labor sustain a providential history and the old law, but also confirm the world as it is, groaning under the weight of secularized religion. From his birth, Samson's faith has been conveyed by a prescriptive dependency, one discontinuous with significant procreation for him and without marital reconciliation. The sterile, unloving imagery of a deserted night with which he characterizes his blindness—its contradiction of God's prime, generating decree—also displays the inescapable moral ambiguity of his life's results. Moreover, the "Ease to the body" provided by Dagon's holiday and the attempts of the Philistines to associate his strength with play and entertaining are travesties of the legitimate day of rest sanctioned by the law and by Genesis. The festivities are telling caricatures of Samson's prospects; like Dalila's proposed bliss "At home in leisure and domestic ease" (line 917), the masquerades veil yet ironically reveal his degradation. The actual consequence of such promiscuous mingling of insight with distraction would be yet more slavery.

The day of rest can be one of fruitful consequence in true religion, of course, preserving the continuity of repentance, faith, and love in the consciousness of the faithful, and here the excesses of the Philistine holiday implicitly contrast with the stability of the Mosaic Sabbath. But both holidays allude to the "dangerous tendency"—in the caution of Milton's Independent disciplinary attitude—toward an established Sabbath in the contemporary church. In true religion, the reformed Sabbath should be regarded as a condition of right-minded choice, as an edifying freedom from prescribed, temporal religion. Like compulsory tithing, keeping the Sabbath is not moral or godly in itself; rather, "the seaventh day is not moral, but a convenient recourse of worship in fit season" (*Considerations Touching the Likeliest Means,* in Yale Prose, 7:295). Calvin, too, citing Col. 2:16–17, comments that the Sabbath of the old law was "'a shadow of what is to come; but the body belongs to Christ,' that is, the very substance of truth." Christ's coming overwhelms "all figures," including that of the Sabbath, and Christians must "shun completely the superstitious observance of days." Instead of being regarded as "confined within a single day," the Sabbath should be seen as extending "through the whole course of our life, until, completely dead to ourselves, we are filled with the life of God."[12]

On his travestied day of rest, Samson's strongest antagonist is his turbulent state of mind, a stinging guilt, with which cultural experience, Philistine or Danite, seems discontinuous. In desperation, he reaches for shadowy possibilities of deliverance as means to reestablish a heroic identity—the guiding hand, the match with Harapha, the pillars "Felt in his arms" (line

1636). His depressed intuition, however, is greater than the dialogues or the challenges at hand can meet. When Dalila asks him, "Let me approach at least, and touch thy hand," he reacts demonstratively: "Not for thy life, lest fierce remembrance wake / My sudden rage to tear thee joint by joint" (lines 951–53). This imagined figure of himself as well as of her, one fruitlessly commensurate with her "Matrimonial treason" (line 959), sustains the mutuality of sin and desire as a divisive memory—a personal history, like that of ecclesiastical history, nurturing an explosive, defensive egoism.

In *Paradise Lost*, after Adam and Eve have been tragically subdued by selfish love, the guiding hand is that of Michael, then of "Providence," whose presence is felt not only as an inner mood of reconciliation but also as the bodily touch, "hand in hand," of wife and husband entering the fallen world. The foresight needed for a sanctified life in the world as it is—a place where Samson may be rightly perceived as a necessary but not sufficient kind of deliverer—is in *Paradise Lost* choreographed by marital reconciliation. Adam and Eve's providential communion is a second garden, a nurturing paradigm of right-minded religion, a figure of the mystical body as well as a material preparation for the promised Seed. Their reformed marriage conveys the structure of true religion as "unanimous," and Michael accordingly enjoins Adam—the tragic, yet epic, hero—to reveal, not withhold, from Eve, the heroine, his secret, the good news to be spoken with authority:

> Let her with thee partake what thou hast heard,
> Chiefly what may concern her Faith to know,
> The great deliverance by her Seed to come
> (For by the Womans Seed) on all Mankind.
> That ye may live, which will be many dayes,
> Both in one Faith unanimous though sad,
> With cause for evils past, yet much more cheer'd
> With meditation on the happie end.
>
> (*P.L.*, XII.598–605)

This expanded perspective of the "happie end," one that subordinates both forbidden knowledge and "All secrets of the deep, all Natures works" (XII.578), conditions the mood and discipline of worship. Its inclusiveness may be contrasted with Samson's narrowly cultic secret and the hazard of his unreformed relationship with Dalila; perhaps, too, the epic perspective contrasts with the spending of passion (the last statement of the Danite chorus) in tribal enthusiasm rather than in intimate affection.

In the fallen world, faith can be nurtured by love and by an informed contemplation of history. Yet, as Michael's guidance reveals, an original right-mindedness about the mutuality of procreation, patriarchy, and adoration will be confused by further disobedience and compromised by a self-celebrating egoism displaced as authorized worship. Even Adam's newly repentant, reformed idea of worship first tends in this direction. His prospect of worship in a fallen condition depends on his lingering sense of place and dominion; his regret at seeming to have lost sight of God is initially misinformed by his imagining the practice of worship among sons yet to be born. He laments that he will not be able to show his sons where in Paradise God once appeared to him (XI.319-21) in part because the places of worship will not reflect his precedence so readily as would Paradise. The error is superstitious, and, as Fowler notes, the passage also alludes to the "narrow bounds of the institutional church."[13] Adam hopes to transfer religious authority to his sons, but the intention is compromised by a psychology associating the image of God with high places, perhaps a significance more phallic than nurturing, as suggested by the presumed sanctity of "Mount," "Tree," and "Pines" (XI.320–21). Michael here corrects Adam's patriarchal imagination by referring him instead to the divine Father's unbounded love, a "paternal Love," to be sure, but also a nurturing kind of fatherhood, an image of God more abundant and suffusing than Adam's lost "praeeminence" (XI.347, 353). Michael's more encompassing perspective implies God's ubiquitous energy—"all the Earth: / Not this Rock onely"—and includes a maternal, cooperative mood that recalls that of the Spirit's brooding in the epic's first invocation (I.19–26): "His Omnipresence fills / Land, Sea, and Aire, and every kinde that lives, / Fomented by his virtual power and warmd" (XI.335–38).

Michael's edifying correction of the nature of worship anticipates his later distinction between the "works of Law" and the "works of Faith" that supersede them in the new covenant (XII.302–6). He allows that "Law can discover sin" in the world of the "shadowie expiations weak" of ceremonial Judaism (XII.290–92), expiations "informing" the faithful, moreover, of "the destind Seed" (XII.232–33). In contrast, a fully informed understanding of sin and of providential destiny is obscured by liturgical spectacle. The theatrical connotation of "shadowie expiations" gives the lie to the supposed efficacy of acting out purification without the authority of a prior reconciliation with the Father. A hero of the old law, Samson would convey an ironic typology of difference for the Christian reader, as William Madsen has noted.[14] The better covenant of the Gospel and its Old

Testament analogue of familial love is a more securely articulated text for the practice of worship than one calling for "The bloud of Bulls and Goats." As this sequence of animal imagery implies, the ritual form of such sacrifice is bathetic, ironically revealing a culture's lack of rightly reasoned discipline. Rather, the right-minded aesthetic of commemorative sacrifice—and Milton is probably alluding to contemporary church discipline as well—is "disciplin'd / From shadowie Types to Truth, from Flesh to Spirit" (XII.302–3). This better work of the people, or true liturgy, has the clarity of the actual; it is more fully realized even though the sensuousness of its ceremony has been significantly reduced. Eventually, the covenant can be expressed by "works of Faith" rather than of law. Then the grace to worship as God's chosen instead of as a patriarch's fearful issue will affect conscience (and the consciousness of sin) with a more edifying kind of awe, as moral psychology shifts its emphasis "from servil fear / To filial" (XII.305–6).

The promise of a less theatrical (or histrionic) and a more mature psychology of worship figured as freely chosen reverence of the Father is consistent with *Paradise Lost*'s great mystery of the Father's union with the Son, which was first choreographed not only by angels in heaven but also by the "Rites / Mysterious of connubial Love" in the garden's "inmost bower," and by the "adoration pure" at its threshold (IV.737–43). Here, worship was continuous with intimacy, uninhibited by sin or by the boundaries of egoism. The mutual gestures of Adam and Eve, a blissful ceremony of unfallen minds and bodies, celebrated their covenant with the Father and with each other, and expressed their choice of the good privately as well as outside the threshold. Their right-minded manner of worship was procreative in every sense. Their deeds are later shadowed by the "disport" and "amorous" play of sexual activity not yet fully informed (or reformed) by sober reflection (IX.1034ff.), but the legacy of an uncorrupted performance of love as worship is an implicit part of the paradise to be regained and to be expressed as works of faith. Michael's peroration to Adam therefore implies a cumulatively exalted future, a life and works that include tragic as well as epic and pastoral kinds of history: "onely add / Deeds to thy knowledge answerable, . . . (XII.581ff.).

Filial labor, able service by the fallen hero, can approximate a kind of edifying liturgy, one that is acted out in daily life as well as in the practice of worship. Yet servile fear, for Milton, perpetuates the unreformed mood of the prelatical church (eventually the Presbyterian replacement as well), an institution that exhibits the litigious, political characteristics of the old covenant on the one hand and those of a Dagonic cult, the Roman Church, on the other. In *The Reason of Church Government*, he had observed that contemporary church discipline and liturgy, which should be included in the works of faith, are rather agents of tyranny:

> The service of God who is Truth, her Liturgy confesses to be perfect freedom, but her works and her opinions declare that the service of Prelaty is perfect slavery, and by consequence perfect falsehood. (Yale Prose, 1:854)

Liturgy has been corrupted, invalidated by motives for power, and what may seem the design of prescribed ritual actually demonstrates disorder, a deformed performance, to right-minded Christians:

> 'Tis not the goodnesse of matter therefore which is not, nor can be ow'd to the *Liturgie*, that will beare it out, if the form, which is the essence of it, be fantastick, and superstitious, the end sinister, and the imposition violent. (Yale Prose, 1:688)

Instead, as stated in *De Doctrina*, "the true worship of God is eagerness to do good works." This is because "faith, as form, gives form to the works, so that they can be good." The mutuality of terms in metaphysics and theology in the humanist tradition that Milton follows reiterates the premise of reformed worship: "Faith, then, is the form of good works, because the definition of *form* is *that through which a thing is what it is*" (Yale Prose, 6:637, 639).[15] Hence, from Milton's position, affective, unprescribed liturgy (perhaps even the iconoclastic works of reformers) is not formless, even though form in the conventionally aesthetic sense is not evident. Because of right motive, the essential form of prayer and of liturgical discipline is decorous, as he argues in *An Apology for Smectymnuus:*

> Certainly Readers, the worship of God singly in it selfe, the very act of prayer and thanksgiving with those free and unimpos'd expressions which from a sincere heart unbidden come into the outward gesture, is the greatest decency that can be imagin'd. Which to dresse up and garnish with a devis'd bravery abolisht in the law, and disclaim'd by the Gospell adds nothing but a deformed uglinesse. (Yale Prose, 1:941–42)

However, as Milton suggests in the *First Defense*, the deeds of reformers can be complicated by tragic effects and obscured by their own uncharitable, egoistic motives. Speaking of Samson, he observes:

Yet against those Philistincs, under whose dominion he was, he himself undertook a war in his own person, without any other help; and whether he acted in pursuance of a command from Heaven, or was prompted by his valour only, or whatever inducement he had, he did not put to death one, but many, that tyrannized over his country, having first called upon God by prayer, and implored his assistance. So that Samson counted it no act of impiety, but quite contrary, to kill those that enslaved his country. (Yale Prose, 4, pt. 1:402)

Milton's main point in this polemical context is that tyrannicide does not require an explicit command from God; Charles Stuart had become an enemy of the people and was justly put to death. Rhetorically, the Samson story can support a high-minded interpretation of English constitutional history. As a supposed type of Christian parable, however, the allusion to Samson is frustratingly terminal. It does not abide as the Gospel does. But we also hear Milton's reformist voice indicating the dramatic potential of Samson—his possible complex of motives, his unclear motives, and his uncooperative kind of courage. The relationship between Samson's deeds and his knowledge will be shadowy in posterity even if clear to himself. His historical ethos will be perpetually mixed, which is a likely destiny of heroic narrative lacking Gospel authority.

In *Samson Agonistes*, a similar discrepancy between fateful, necessary events and their unstable significance eventuates in a diverting but actually uninformed celebration. There is a general "law" of "dire necessity" (*S.A.*, line 1666), the people declare, a mortal catastrophe from which Samson could not have escaped. At the same time, they believe that God has intentionally sent "the spirit of phrenzie," which stimulates the "mad desire" of the Philistines to call for Samson's performance, and so "thir own ruin on themselves t' invite" (lines 1675, 1677, 1684). Samson's prophesied "work" is thereby "fulfill'd" (lines 1661–62). This makes patriotic sense, but does not commemorate sufficiently the universal heritage of sin. For the Chorus, the Philistines' festive diversions, the entertainment and the polity expressing their degeneration, are instead subsumed by God's "uncontroulable intent" (line 1754), taken as the cause of temporal history. First "unsearchable," then perceivable "in the close" (lines 1746, 1754), the divine plan itself can be gratifying, lending authorized form to hermeneutics and to history. But, while Samson's final deed is in his view within the context of the Hebrew law (lines 1408–9), at the same time it is derived from his resistance to further humiliation. His statement to the Officer— "Because they shall not trail me through thir streets / Like a wild Beast, I am content to go" (lines 1402–3)—is ironically manipulative yet vainly expressive.

Milton therefore dramatizes the temporary sanction of the law and its complex historical function "to evince . . . natural depravitie," as Michael had told Adam, "by stirring up / Sin against Law to fight" (*P.L.,* XII.288–89). The law, like Samson in the dramatic context, may be edifyingly construed as opposed to sin, but its victory is temporary or temporal. Indeed, as Bennet also remarks, the paradox of Samson's obligation to a law that is impossible to keep reveals the law's weakness.[16] It does not "remove" sin; it offers "peace / Of conscience," but it "cannot appease," according to Michael in *Paradise Lost.* Essentially, the law and Hebrew ceremony are incomplete forms. Their Miltonic function is, in a general sense, deconstructive—again, their "purpose to resign them in full time / Up to a better Cov'nant, disciplin'd / From shadowie Types to Truth . . ." (*P.L.,* XII.287–303). The form of Samson's heroism is imperfect, because "Man" cannot "the moral part / Perform, and not performing cannot live. / So Law appears imperfet . . ."(XII.297–300). The festive theater of Manoa's imagination may generate "matchless valour, and adventures high" (*S.A.,* line 1740) among God's servants laboring under the old law, but this ceremonial will be associated with ancestral bones—jealously guarded, territorial reminders of place. Manoa's pronouncement, "*Samson* hath quit himself / Like *Samson,* and heroicly hath finish'd / A life Heroic" (lines 1709–11) implies a patriarch's wish for culture as a closed form, its heroism "finish'd" or perfected and therefore constituting an inspiring historical text. The tautological figure, "himself / Like *Samson,*" however, unintentionally temporalizes inspiration; the simile weds Samson's deeds to self-aggrandizement and tribalism, to the likeness or shadow of true religion rather than its actual body.

Manoa's final preference for the likeness of a Samson who existed prior to the reality of his son's tragic figure echoes the greater error of Dagon's worshipers. The theatrical design of their temple and ceremonies encourages a licentious, ungodly religion, to be sure, but Milton also refers us to the cultural hazard of promoting any religion by means of theaters of worship, by the likeness of piety as a means to empowerment even within divinely authorized religion. The Messenger tells Manoa that Samson first performed "as a public servant brought / In their state Livery clad" (lines 1616–17) when he was taken to the temple, "a spacious Theatre / Half round on two main Pillars vaulted high" (lines 1605–6). This structure of Milton's devising, as readers often notice, is reminiscent of playhouses such as the Globe or the Curtain. Under the roofed portion supported by the pillars, the "choice nobility and flower" of the kingdom, "Lords, Ladies, Captains, Councellors, or Priests," sit (lines 1653–54). The common throng, among whom the Messenger himself "aloof obscurely stood," are "On banks and scaffolds" in the open side of the theater (lines 1609–11). They will escape the crushing fate of their leaders and of Samson because Samson's gesture is concentrated against the pillars of the establishment.[17]

The Philistines, celebrating the authority of Dagon, or attempting to authorize their own moral disorder, would see their captive hero act out his awesome strength according to a solemn, prescriptive scenario. The theatrical aesthetic enforced by the priests and the Officer commanding Samson's presence would beautify the dirty, downtrodden figure of the mill house, while at the same time it would commemorate their relegating the mighty judge to slavery. In turn, their solemn plan for cultural aggrandizement gives Samson the opportunity to subdue them violently. His ironic play within the play lures the Philistines off their guard and enables him to touch the pillars. Pretending exhaustion, he asks to "lean a while / With both his arms," then announces,

> Hitherto, Lords, what your commands impos'd
> I have perform'd, as reason was, obeying,
> Not without wonder or delight beheld.
> Now of my own accord such other tryal
> I mean to shew you of my strength, yet greater;
> As with amaze shall strike all who behold.
>
> (lines 1640–45)

The promise of a spectacle of strength, and its vicarious transfer of power to the Philistine lords watching, is ironically an appeal to weakness in Samson's oppressors—their appetite for powerful spectacle, Samson intuitively perceives, will relax their guard. His verbal irony and sarcasm imply the power of another secret: his duplicity and his recovered strength, and the force of its timely revelation by means of destruction. That he now proposes feats of strength of his "own accord" might seem the enthusiasm of a braggart hoping to elicit applause, and, before they are crushed by the debris of the temple, the Philistines succumb to the rhetoric of theatrical performance or public sport.

Samson himself cannot escape this hazard of performance allied to prayer. The question of his authorship and motive remains ironic because of the nature of prescriptive ceremony—there are grounds for various interpretations of the event in the minds of its participants, both before and after the catastrophe. Enacting an interpretation of the old law weakens rather than strengthens definitive statement, even if authorship of the law itself remains clear. Hence, Samson's performance also lessens the authoritative significance of the law, an irony dramatically anticipated in his farewell to the Chorus:

> Be of good courage, I begin to feel
> Some rouzing motions in me which dispose
> To something extraordinary my thoughts.
> I with this Messenger will go along,
> Nothing to do, be sure, that may dishonour
> Our Law, or stain my vow of *Nazarite.*
> If there be aught of presage in the mind,
> This day will be remarkable in my life
> By some great act, or of my days the last.
>
> (lines 1381–89)

The salutary promise, "Be of good courage," is not fulfilled but frustrated by the lack of omniscient narrative clarity in "rouzing motions" and the obscurity of "some great act" motivated by them. His reference to the law is an appeal to objective authority in order to establish his role in the cultic body, but it is also an exculpatory statement prompted by desperation. The absolutist tone—"This day will be remarkable in my life / By some great act, or of my days the last"—implies the lonely subjectivity of his magisterial behavior, a shadow of authorized deliverance, measured by "days" rather than by timelessness. His assertion is heroic, but in the sense whereby a hero is fixed in time, his fame perennially subject to historical reputation and to the kind of commemorative gestures that will be, or should be, outmoded. His degree of "presage" is therefore conditioned by a consciousness of sin but limited by its cultic reference, rather than liberated by reformed, independent religion. There is nobility here, but also the "last infirmity of Noble mind" once evident in the initially misinformed elegist's response to Lycidas's death in Milton's pastoral elegy (*Lycidas,* line 71). The consequences of his awesome labor—apparent freedom and iconoclasm—invite celebration among the cultic body but do not clarify the timeless body of true religion.

In the marital union that is the center of the tragedy, and that suggests a crisis of the old law, Samson's cultic pledge had stimulated possessiveness rather than love, an effect that weakens his spiritual authority as husband. His relationship with Dalila had not been fruitful in issue or in affective expression. His memory of laying the cultic secret in her lap (*S.A.,* line 535) ironically alludes to reclaiming a fallen identity rather than issuing from it. "[I] unbosom'd all my secrets to thee . . . who could deny thee nothing," he also recalls to her, but as a consequence he was unable to lead her into his own domain (lines 879–900).

Dalila's festive costume, her entering the action "With all her bravery on, and tackle trim" (line 717), reveals a weakened domestic authority on her part. Unlike Milton's Eve, as Ricki Heller has pointed out, Dalila appears immodest and unrepentant, her attitude contrasting suggestively with the edifying, conjugal devotion of Adam's wife.[18] The secret has not empowered her in her relationship with him. The sarcastic, rhetorical question of the Chorus, "But who is this, what thing of Sea or Land? / Femal of sex it seems" (lines 710–11), indirectly implies her dependence on Dagon, the amphibious idol, and points to the theatrical limitation of meretricious sexuality: its tendency to undermine informed reconciliation. The potential of her awareness of mutual guilt ("Let weakness then with weakness come to parl" [line 785]) and her offer of romantic servitude to Samson are accordingly heard by him as rhetorically monstrous—to him, her terms, "expiate," "penance," and "pardon" are prompted by "malice not repentance" (line 821); hers must be "feign'd Religion, smooth hypocrisie" (line 871). In her confused and eventually combative mood, she is a reflection of him, and he may intuit his image in her confronting him. Actual love, "as it ought, sincere," he argues—perhaps against himself as well as her—"would have taught thee / Far other reasonings, brought forth other deeds" than pleas of civic and religious duty (lines 873–75). The security she does promise with "forgiveness" would be succeeded, in her account, by sensual "delights," even "though sight be lost" (lines 911–16), which suggests a future that sounds more enervating than reforming or fruitful in this context. Here the shadow of love would merely extend the Philistine holiday for Samson.

Dalila's love, of course, is pathetically devoid of spiritual gifts or grace, even though she may merit our sympathy as the recipient of Samson's anger and denigration. We can also recall, as Samson apparently does not, the consequences of the tragic fall in the context of Adam and Eve's marriage, where reasonings and deeds were affected by grace and where the pathos of human love was subsumed by the epic mystery of divine love. Unlike Adam and Eve, Samson and Dalila are not inspired lovers; their temporal union is discontinuous with the mystical body. Eve's supplicating approach to Adam, "I beg, and clasp thy knees" (*P.L.,* X.918), is both disarming and illuminating; it presents a true dialogue of weakness with weakness and undermines pride. Her naked honesty is divested of amorous "play" (IX. 1027). The prospect of reconciliation is informed by grief rather than misinformed by it, and their repentance summarizes a comprehensive history of the tragic past, worshipful present, and redemptive future:

> they forthwith to the place
> Repairing where he judg'd them prostrate fell
> Before him reverent, and both confess'd
> Humbly their faults, and pardon beg'd, with tears
> Watering the ground, and with thir sighs the Air
> Frequenting, sent from hearts contrite, in sign
> Of sorrow unfeign'd, and humiliation meek.
>
> (X.1098–1104)

Dalila, with good reason, finally strikes the attitude of a marital victor, then compares her imagined infamy in Israel with her fame in Gaza. In Samson's domain, she will be cursed and "Of falsehood most unconjugal traduc't" (*S.A.,* line 979), but in her own country she will be "nam'd among the famousest / Of Women, sung at solemn festivals" (lines 981–82). She appreciates the margins of fame, and its "double mouth'd" temporality (lines 972–74), but, in her grief, she grasps for the narrower victory of fame. Similarly, Samson is at first cynical about the famous roll of initially misunderstood Hebrew leaders—the list of popular history to which he will be added—then confident of "God's proposed deliverance" (lines 277–92), but he is ultimately drawn to a temporal victory. In the temple, performing first histrionically and then demonstratively, Samson is like Dalila.

The sterile resolution of marital struggle in *Samson Agonistes* underlines the dramatic poem's contest between affective, internal worship and cultic performance, the theater of worship. Samson and Dalila will not consummate a reconciliation—the charitable deeds or expression of forgiveness—because of the displaced egoism unhappily serving as culture. Dalila's approach to him touches the still-trembling nerve of Samson's cultic identity, his pride, and he will not again be disarmed. He rejects the plea of mutual "weakness" and rhetorically equates weakness with wickedness itself (lines 831–34). The Chorus, too, obscures the worthier struggle—that of reconciliation and its mysterious choreography of the relationship of their sinful character to the Father—when they elaborate on the hazard of uxoriousness as a defense of male despotism:

> Therefore Gods universal law
> Gave to the man despotic power
> Over his female in due awe,
> Nor from that right to part an hour,
> Smile she or lowr;
> So shall he least confusion draw
> On his whole life, not sway'd
> By female usurpation, nor dismay'd.
>
> (lines 1053–60)

The cultural sanction of "Gods universal Law" by the Chorus impedes the mysteriously charitable rite of love, even though, like established religion, the sanction has some claim to social and moral clarity. Samson himself trusts in God's forgiveness, and later he asserts as much to Harapha (lines 1171–72), but he cannot, or will not, trust himself to enact the gestures of forgiveness. He expects that God's "ear is ever open" to the suppliant (line 1172), but his own comprehensive knowledge of sin results in a severe defensiveness: "So much of Adders wisdom I have learn't / To fence my ear against thy sorceries" (lines 936–37). In turn, Dalila's proposed gesture of reconciliation (951), ignites his violent imagination; the memory of intimacy as betrayal and as weakness angers him to the point of wishing to dismember her (lines 952–53), although her bodily presence might also signify the prospect of tragically informed love. His fierce distance maintains the shadow of religion, as does his presumptive, egoistic statement to the Chorus, "So let her go, God sent her to debase me, / And aggravate my folly" (lines 999–1000). The significance of her presence is demeaned by Samson's acknowledgment of folly, whereby he assumes a possessive authoring of her role in his life that is continuous with his owning the secret itself, the "most sacred trust / Of secresie" that is "my safety, and my life" (lines 1001–2). His dismissal of her repossesses history on his own terms: "Love quarrels oft in pleasing concord end, / Not wedlock-trechery endangering life" (lines 1008–9). Neither character will let go of the cultic family and its reenactments of the past. In one sense, tribal structures magnify Samson and Dalila as more than a husband and a wife, but in another these boundaries obscure and diminish the spiritual potential of mutual grief.

The encounter with Harapha is a similarly fruitless exercise in the assertion of cultural authority. "His habit carries peace," the Chorus tells

Samson, "his brow defiance" (line 1073), which recalls their description of Dalila's mixed, or promiscuous, bearing. Harapha's inconsistency in turn magnifies the weakness and probable cowardice of the Philistines on this festival day, an irony also possible in his expression, "the glory of Prowess," and in the supposed authority he could have "recover'd" from the "unforskinn'd race" had he met Samson on the field (lines 1098–1100). Their verbal combat again sustains the shadows of religion. Harapha attacks Samson for presuming God's aid, and when Samson replies that he "despair[s] not," that his God's "ear is ever open; and his eye / Gracious to re-admit the suppliant" (lines 1168–73), he reveals the course of rightly informed worship: a suppliant's plea prompted by hope and by the recognition of divine justice in personal tragedy. To "despair not," however, suggests an imperfect kind of hope, understandably less than "hope" construed in true religion as the corollary of faith in the revealed Christ, and perhaps less than the "devout affection" of hope that is part of internal worship.[19] "Confidence," too, may refer us indirectly to a typology of saving faith, but it is applied by Samson to the limited frame of secular heroism and its tribal sanction:

> In confidence whereof I once again
> Defie thee to the trial of mortal fight,
> By combat to decide whose god is God,
> Thine or whom I with *Israel's* Sons adore.

(lines 1174–77)

If we recall Samson's earlier statement to the Chorus, "Mee easily mine may neglect, / But Gods propos'd deliverance not so" (lines 291–92), we can again sense the way that the underlying frustration of the intuitive, fideistic hero is relegated to cultural ironies; we can see him as one who is identified textually as a timely deliverer, rather than as one who delivers his people from time and from tribal necessity. The dubious outcome of religious dependency in combat and in history can be compared to Manoa's lament, "Nay what thing good / Pray'd for, but often proves our woe, our bane?" (lines 350–51). Specifically he is referring to his fatherhood wounded by the failures of Samson, but more generally to the consequences of adherence to patriarchal frames for worship. A filial analogue of the patriarchal body, Samson has become a merely cultural spectacle, the pledge that is his hair now a "Vain monument of strength" to himself, "redundant locks / Robustious to no purpose clustring down" (lines 568–70). His earlier prayer is a similarly misinformed, fruitless reflection of grief:

> Nor am I in the list of them that hope;
> Hopeless are all my evils, all remediless;
> This one prayer yet remains, might I be heard,
> No long petition, speedy death,
> The close of all my miseries, and the balm.

(lines 647–51)

The prayer that expresses Samson's despair also defines a son's identity as closed, his authority inseparable from a mood of cultic alienation.

The Chorus echoes Manoa's disappointment when they complain about an unpredictable providence, destiny "so various" and "contrarious" (lines 668–69), but their prayer eventually is for God to ensure the significance of Samson's work for them. While they may be fearful and wishful thinkers, they also intuit the importance of opening the mind to mysteriously authorized labor:

> So deal not with this once thy glorious Champion,
> The Image of thy strength, and mighty minister.
> What do I beg? How hast thou dealt already?
> Behold him in this state calamitous, and turn
> His labours, for thou canst, to peaceful end.

(lines 705–9)

Their prayer is also nurture, a ministry to Samson that is a plea for the application of strength to a procreative spirit among the faithful—the "peaceful end" later implied by their observing how a "calm of mind" has been acquired by "passion spent" on Samson's part in the temple (lines 1755–58). But, even if the conversion of labor to peaceful end would be celebrated on "feastful days" according to Manoa's plan (line 1741), these final images of worship are occasional and do not share in the substance of future events. Samson's passion is spent not in marital reconciliation or in procreation but in iconoclasm.

Manoa, too, would rather reclaim the "accidental" history of Samson for an enclosed, patriarchal context. For him, "a worse thing" than violating the secret is the seeming authority his son has lent to the Philistines' "popular Feast / Here celebrate in Gaza" (lines 433–35). This shame to "thy Fathers house" (line 447) may be compensated by paying the Philistines a ransom, enabling Samson's "filial submission" when he would return "Home to thy countrey and his [God's] sacred house" (lines 511, 518). There, God's "further ire" might be turned aside by Samson's "praiers and

vows renew'd" (line 520). Implicitly, the authority associated with the secret would be restored through a father's agency, through submission rather
than filial love, and worship would be relegated to preserving ancestral
boundaries. Ironically, however, Manoa's near success in ransom ("with
supplication prone and Fathers tears" [line 1459]) and the Chorus's agree-
ment that such "hopes are not ill-founded nor seem vain" (line 1504) are
simultaneous with the shattering of these syntaxes of culture. The "hideous
noise" from the temple (line 1509) and Manoa's diplomatic scheme are
overwhelmed by what seems more eventful: a sudden collapse of national-
ist structure. The line that precedes also splits rhetorically between the choral
listeners and Manoa's spontaneous exclamation: "I know your friendly
minds and—O what noise!" (line 1508).

At this point, a psychology of redemption is possible, one that is better
communicated in the initially traumatized but perceptive witness of the
Messenger. The Messenger's arrival and panic-stricken speech dramatize
an affective source of authority, one that is at first beyond Manoa's rhetoric:

> O whither shall I run, or which way flie
> The sight of this so horrid spectacle
> Which earst my eyes beheld and yet behold;
> For dire imagination still persues me?
>
> (lines 1541–44)

The Messenger's "dire imagination," his dramatic moment of witness,
is analogous as well to Milton's predicament as a dramatic poet. The ethos
of Samson has been subsumed by events; his motives, as Milton recognized in the *First Defense*, are irreducible or at least ambivalent ("a command from Heaven . . . his valour only, or whatever inducement he had"
[Yale Prose 4, pt. 1:402]). Like the reformer's witness to the biblical event,
i.e., to the text of that event, the Messenger's witness is independent, if
also furiously imagined. Still, for the Messenger, this assertion of a paradoxical yet enthusiastic self is soon deferred by his returning to patriarchal
boundaries of meaning:

> But providence or instinct of nature seems,
> Or reason though disturb'd, and scarse consulted
> T' have guided me aright, I know not how,
> To thee first reverend *Manoa*, and to these
> My Countreymen, whom here I knew remaining.
>
> (lines 1545–49)

His now less intuitive and more rhetorical "sense" of the catastrophe is in turn encouraged by Manoa: "Tell us the sum, the circumstance defer" (line 1557). The event that has tragically defeated Manoa's intentions—that in addition to the Philistines, Samson too is dead—is shifted to circumstance, delayed by the Messenger as a "too rude irruption / Hitting thy aged ear," and the "sum" of his report—"*Gaza* yet stands, but all her Sons are fall'n"— conditioned by his relationship to the father and to country. Unconscious routes to self-preservation are continuous with unreformed religion, and the Messenger is drawn to Manoa because in time and space he has no- where else to go, no pastures new and fresh woods.

Perhaps the establishmentarian tendency in rhetoric and religion can help put the fears of messengers and historians to rest, but ultimately this tendency is prescriptive and condescending, a psychology of religion that enervates the force of witness. Manoa, understandably, would modify the prospect of Samson's own demonstration of disturbed reason, natural in- stinct, and providential strength by inviting a circumstantial history of more strictly edifying proportions than the Messenger has seen: "Yet e're I give the rains to grief, say first, / How dy'd he? death to life is crown or shame" (lines 1578–79). The details, however, that Samson died by his "own hands" rather than by an opponent's "glorious hand" (lines 1584, 1581), ironically enhance the elusive aspect of Samson's ethos in the Messenger's lengthier description (lines 1596ff.). This characterization of Samson—narrated by the common believer, the potential liturgist who "sorrow'd at his captive state, but minded / Not to be absent at that spectacle" (lines 1603–4)—is like that of Milton's reference in the *First Defense*. Both contexts empha- size the hero's violent energy, but take no position on the issue of motive: "And eyes fast fixt he stood, as one who pray'd, / Or some great matter in his mind revolv'd" (lines 1637–38). The Chorus, too, reciprocates Manoa's intention and lyrically magnifies Samson's glory as prophetically reveal- ing God's glory:

> O dearly-bought revenge, yet glorious!
> Living or dying thou hast fulfill'd
> The work for which thou wast foretold
> To *Israel*, and now ly'st victorious
> Among the slain self-kill'd
> Not willingly, but tangl'd in the fold
> Of dire necessity. . . .

(1660–66)

The celebratory lyricism of the Chorus and Manoa's prospect of "copious Legend" and "sweet Lyric Song" at Samson's future monument (line 1737) summarize the tendency of establishmentarian liturgy. Mythography and aestheticism in the contexts of grief ensure the preservation of culture, and lend significance to catastrophe. As readers also notice, the last song of the Chorus, the *exodos* of Milton's dramatic poem, approximates a sonnet (lines 1745–58), a closed prosody that breathes consolation, closure. But, at the same time, the *exodos* begs the question of an ending: what is "ever best found in the close" (line 1748) is not, of course, *the* close, but the end of a tragic episode. In its spent passion, the episode still invites presumption along with "calm of mind" (line 1758). The mood and prospect are circumstantially beautiful, but shadows of true religion.

In his preface to *Samson Agonistes*, Milton argues that tragedy as a contemporary cultural expression is also a kind of vanity, an entertainment absurdly mixed and therefore lacking in essential form and significance. His renovated dramatic form will be an "essential" kind of tragedy, one that does not follow a choral prosody originally "fram'd only for Music" and now "not essential to the Poem," but instead a kind that is overall free from trivial theatricalism. The best kind of chorus, he specifies, is "not antient only but modern," and the "modelling" of the work, too, may be referred to both "the Antients and *Italians*," which implies an aesthetic outside of time yet a keen awareness of the tendency of popular taste and the academic authority of literary history. The new aesthetic is derived from the errors as well as the better motives of the past and the present; it reflects a sense of form that is comparable to attitudes of worship free from vain aestheticism. In the Argument's synopsis, we are told that Samson was "at length perswaded inwardly" that the command for him to perform in the temple "was from God." Yet this is the tone of limited omniscience, a detachment consistent with Milton's remark, "whatever inducement he [Samson] had," in the *First Defense*. The "essential" history of Samson may have the informing potential of parabolic literature—a contradictory and unexpected kind of narrative—which opposes mythography and thereby opens the mind to inspired truth, although in itself it is not paradigmatic history. Such were the parables Jesus told.[20] In Milton's dramatic poem, the extrabiblical witness, the Messenger, begins to narrate the parabolic event. The elder Manoa, however, who reviews history with dim awareness, and the Chorus who commemorate prior expectation, confuse cultural redundancy with insight. Among reformers, the otherwise celebratory statement, "*Samson* hath quit himself / Like *Samson*," is also a cause for grief.

Unhappily, as Milton's tragic context implies, an institutionalized mythology of "Holy Revenge" is questioned less over time, and reformist insights are obscured by commemorative celebration rather than illuminated by the interrogating force of prophetic witness. Such is one predictable trend in statist religions now as well as in the seventeenth century. Perhaps seeing the cultural ironies and hazards of establishmentarian worship in *Samson Agonistes* can still serve as a contemporary, cautionary criticism of religious nationalism blindly empowered.

Notes

PREFACE

1. Milton's authorship of the treatise has been challenged recently by William B. Hunter but defended by a number of scholars—perhaps most forcefully by Christopher Hill—as in fact Milton's own work and consistent with his other prose writings. William B. Hunter, "The Provenance of the *Christian Doctrine*," *Studies in English Literature* 32 (1992): 129–42, 163–66; idem, "The Provenance of the *Christian Doctrine:* Addenda from the Bishop of Salisbury," *Studies in English Literature* 33 (1993): 191–207; idem, "Animadversions upon the Remonstrants' Defense against Burgess and Hunter," *Studies in English Literature* 34 (1994): 195–203. Christopher Hill, "Professor William B. Hunter, Bishop Burgess, and John Milton," *Studies in English Literature* 34 (1994): 165–93. In the most recent of his three articles listed here, Hunter does not dispute Milton's "connection" with the treatise but rather his authorship, a question that needs answering "so that we can evaluate how to employ it in interpreting his work" (202, 203 n. 2).

2. The earlier versions are as follows:
"*Lycidas:* Hurled Bones and the Noble Mind of Reformed Congregations," *Milton Studies* 26 (1991): 59–80. James D. Simmonds, ed., copyright 1991 by University of Pittsburgh Press. Reprinted by permission of the publisher.

"Milton's Twenty-Third Sonnet: Love, Death, and the Mystical Body of the Church," *Milton Quarterly* 24, no. 1 (1990): 8–20. Reprinted by permission of the editor, Roy C. Flannagan.

"'True Religion' and Tragedy: Milton's Insights in *Samson Agonistes*," *Mosaic* 28, no. 3 (1995): 1–29. Reprinted by permission of the editor, Evelyn J. Hinz.

INTRODUCTION

1. *The Complete Prose Works of John Milton*, ed. Don M. Wolfe (New Haven: Yale University Press, 1953–82), vol. 4, pt. 1:322, 511, 636. Further references to this edition are cited parenthetically as Yale Prose.

Masson concludes that Milton's religious practice was eventually one "resembling rather the vague Independency that Cromwell represented, and that was rife in the Army."

David Masson, *The Life of John Milton: Narrated in Connexion With the Political, Ecclesiastical, and Literary History of His Time*, vol. 3 (1859–94; reprint, Gloucester, Mass.: Peter Smith, 1965), 286. Parker cites the claim in John Toland's early biography (1698) on Milton's mature religion that he "was not a professed member of any particular sect among Christians, he frequented none of their assemblies, nor made use of their peculiar rites in his family." William Riley Parker, *Milton: A Biography* (Oxford: Clarendon Press, 1968), 1:579. Of course, like many Independents and sectarians, Milton was at times officially compliant with the Church of England. In his twenties, he was a reform-minded Anglican, as Nathaniel Henry has pointed out, a more radical Independent in his middle years, and in his later years nominally "at peace" with the restored Anglican Church. Henry's conclusion that "Milton was a conforming member of the national episcopal church forty-four of his sixty-six years," and that "his Puritanism was that of the Church of England" may overstate this case, however. Nathaniel Henry, *The True Wayfaring Christian: Studies in Milton's Puritanism* (New York: Peter Lang, 1987), 3, 31.

    2. See Masson, *Life of Milton,* 4:566, 2:573.

    3. Quoted in Michael Fixler, *Milton and the Kingdoms of God* (Chicago: Northwestern University Press, 1964), 120.

    4. Henry Burton, *A Vindication of Churches Commonly Called Independent* (London, 1644), 42.

    5. Don M. Wolfe, *Milton in the Puritan Revolution* (New York and London: Nelson, 1941; reprint, New York: Humanities Press, 1963), 54.

    6. See Christopher Hill, *Milton and the English Revolution* (New York: Viking, 1977), 132, 170.

    7. Burton, *Vindication,* 2.

    8. Ibid., 50, 49.

    9. See Stephen Brachlow, *The Communion of Saints: Radical Puritan and Separatist Ecclesiology, 1570–1625* (Oxford: Oxford University Press, 1988), 114.

    10. Cf. Michael Fixler's observation:

> As his disenchantment extended (and eventually spread very wide), his sense of personal justification became a self-isolating conviction, until at last he stood spiritually alone, a church of one man, as was said of him. . . . only then did he seem easiest in his mind, assured of at least himself as a living temple of faith, and most content to address himself to no particular church but the universal one within which he and his ideal readers . . . communed on that level of Christian understanding that came to serve him as the surrogate for the congregational communion of the church of the visible saints. This was implicitly his posture in the last major poems.

"Ecclesiology," in *A Milton Encyclopedia*, ed. William B. Hunter Jr. et al. (Lewisburg, Pa.: Bucknell University Press, 1978), 2:192.

    The concept of the *ecclesia invisibilia* is outlined in *De Doctrina Christiana* (Yale Prose, 6:498–500), as noted below in my first essay. The term was also used—or perhaps misused—by Anglican bishops for establishmentarian purposes, as Milton critically observes in *Animadversions* (Yale Prose, 1:727).

    On the Calvinist and Lutheran development of "invisible church" as a term signifying the Communion of Saints, and the Roman Catholic responses emphasizing the visible church, see the articles by Avery Dulles, S.J., "Church Membership," in *The Encyclopedia of Religion*, ed. Mircea Eliade (New York: Macmillan, 1987), 3:486–88, and Susan E. Schreiner,

"Church," in *The Oxford Encyclopedia of the Reformation*, ed. Hans Hillerbrand (New York and London: Oxford University Press, 1996), 1:323–27.

11. Fixler, *Milton and the Kingdoms of God*, 272.

12. Ibid., 120.

13. Ibid., 217.

14. Ibid., 170, 109.

15. Sharon Achinstein, *Milton and the Revolutionary Reader* (Princeton: Princeton University Press, 1994), 222.

16. Andrew Marvell, *Complete Poetry*, ed. George deF. Lord (New York: Modern Library, 1968), 56, lines 46–66. Further reference is cited parenthetically in the text by line number.

17. Maryann McGuire, *Milton's Puritan Masque* (Athens: University of Georgia Press, 1983). Cf. Arthur E. Barker's comment on the spiritual significance of the Lady in *Milton and the Puritan Dilemma* (Toronto: University of Toronto Press, 1942), 15.

Fixler, however, finds *Comus* to be a work compromised by Milton's youthful aestheticism, its spiritual didacticism "undercut by the formal requirements of the mask which induce a magical denouement." Here, Milton's poetry is not yet the "really workable moral instrument" that it became with *Lycidas*. *Milton and the Kingdoms of God*, 51.

18. *The Complete Poetry of John Donne*, ed. John T. Shawcross (New York: Anchor Books, 1967), 350, lines 9–14.

19. Quoted in William Riley Parker, *Milton's Contemporary Reputation* (Columbus: Ohio State University Press, 1940), 76–77.

See also N. H. Henry, "Who Meant License When They Cried Liberty," *Modern Language Notes* 66 (1951): 509–13, and Hill, *Milton and the English Revolution*, 130–41. Hill notes, "Mrs. Attaway is an interesting figure, who has been treated rather flippantly by male historians. She encouraged free discussion after her sermons. Like Milton she was a mortalist. She believed that there was no hell save in the conscience . . ." (131).

20. Parker, *Milton's Contemporary Reputation*, 75, 83.

21. The latitudinarian Anglican, George Wither (1588–1667), as well as many other interpreters, regarded Psalms 80–88 as referring to "the estate of the Church, and the Commonwealth of the *Messias*, distinguishing it into her Politicall, Ecclesiasticall, and Oeconomicke Orders" (quoted in Fixler, *Milton and the Kingdoms of God*, 143.

22. William B. Hunter, "Milton Translates the Psalms," *Philological Quarterly* 60 (1961): 485–94.

Chapter 1. Hurled Bones and the Noble Mind

1. Jon S. Lawry, *The Shadow of Heaven: Matter and Stance in Milton's Poetry* (Ithaca: Cornell University Press, 1968), 96–99.

2. Ibid., 101–5.

3. Ibid., 111.

4. Ibid., 118–19.

5. Lawrence W. Hyman, *The Quarrel Within: Art and Morality in Milton's Poetry* (Port Washington, N.Y.: Kennikat Press, 1972), 23.

6. Ibid., 29, 32.

7. Stanley Fish, "*Lycidas*: A Poem Finally Anonymous," in *Milton's "Lycidas": The Tradition and the Poem*, ed. C. A. Patrides (Columbia: University of Missouri Press, 1983), 322, 340.

8. Peter M. Sacks, *"Lycidas,"* in *John Milton: Modern Critical Views*, ed. Harold Bloom (New York: Chelsea House, 1986), 272–74, 279–81.

See also Donald M. Friedman, *"Lycidas*: The Swain's Paideia" on the developing roles of poet and priest, in Patrides, ed., *Milton's "Lycidas,"* 20.

Stewart A. Baker, in his discussion of stylistic levels in the poem, points out that the Orpheus reference "serves as the mythological synthesis for the figures of priest and prophet," and that "the poem itself is ritual," recapturing "the Dionysiac rites of youthful friendship and loss." The poem therefore "celebrates" an "Orphic sensibility." Eventually, the swain undergoes a kind of "transfiguration" when he changes his poetic role for a prophetic one. "Milton's Uncouth Swain," *Milton Studies* 3 (1971): 38–43.

9. See *De Doctrina Christiana*, bk. I, chap. 24, "Of Union and Communion With Christ and His Members, Also of the Mystic or Invisible Church," which cites Romans 12 and 1 Corinthians 12 on the fellowship "through the spirit" of the regenerate with the Father and the Son and with each other, "The Communion of Saints." From Rom. 2:29, this communion is "mystic," "not subject to spatial considerations," and includes people "from all ages since the creation of the world." Well-known figures of the relationship are the church as a household (John 10:14), as one flock protected and taught by Christ the Shepherd (1 Peter 5:4), and as a spousal bond with Christ (Rev. 19:7; Yale Prose, 6:498–500). The church as ship derives from Luke 5:3.

Timothy J. O'Keeffe has surveyed the concept in Milton's prose works in *Milton and the Pauline Tradition: A Study of Theme and Symbolism* (Lanham, Md.: University Press of America, 1982), 203–54. See also Michael Lieb, *The Sinews of Ulysses: Form and Convention in Milton's Works* (Pittsburgh: Duquesne University Press, 1989), 21–37, and idem, *Poetics of the Holy: A Reading of Paradise Lost* (Chapel Hill: University of North Carolina Press, 1981), 38–39. Michael Fixler has analyzed several dimensions of the community of the faithful in *Milton and the Kingdoms of God*. Fixler and Lucretia Bailey Yaghjian in her dissertation, "The Poet and the Church: Visible and Invisible Images of *Ecclesia* in the Early Poetry and Prose of John Milton, 1634–1645" (Ann Arbor, Mich.: University Microfilms, 1976) regard Milton's ecclesiology as evolving from an intent to reform the visible church to an emphasis on the transcendence of the invisible church. More recently, Stephen R. Honeygosky, in *Milton's House of God: The Invisible and Visible Church* (Columbia: University of Missouri Press, 1993) concludes that the two concepts of the church in *De Doctrina* are not opposed. Rather, Milton continually retailors with "new visible characteristics" the very terms of the visible church he denigrates in his polemical writings (234).

In her discussion of *Lycidas*, Yaghjian applies the apocalyptic interpretations of David Pareus (*A Commentary upon the Divine Revelation of the Apostle and the Evangelist* [1644]) to the reformist theme of the poem. Whereas the Lady of *Comus* is a figure of a wandering *ecclesia* moving from invisibility to visibility, Lycidas, associated with the witness of Revelation 11, suggests the measurement of the reformed temple and the authority of the invisible church (Yaghjian, "Poet and the Church," 125, 137).

10. The informal liturgy of Independent and Separatist congregations allowed for members' prophecy as part of the ministry of the word. The famous divine, John Cotton, for example, regarded prophetic exhortation as an important part of regular worship services and of the life of the congregation. See his *The Doctrine of the Church* (London, 1644), 6. This is consistent with Baillie's observation in 1645 that Independents would share the ministry of the word with different members of the congregation contributing to the service, "one to pray, and another to preach, a third to prophecy, and fourth to dismiss, with a

blessing." Quoted in *The Westminster Directory* (Edinburgh and London: William Blackwood and Sons, 1901), 117.

On the significance of the prophetic attitude in *Lycidas*, see William Kerrigan, *The Prophetic Milton* (Charlottesville: University of Virginia Press, 1974), 161–63, 261–62; Joseph Wittreich, *Visionary Poetics: Milton's Tradition and His Legacy* (San Marino, Calif.: Huntington Library Press, 1979), 135–36; and John C. Ulreich Jr., "'And By Occasion Foretells': The Prophetic Voice in *Lycidas*," *Milton Studies* 18 (1983): 3–23.

11. Friedman, "*Lycidas*," 3, comments, "The swain tries to shield himself against the pain of reality by . . . pastoral convention." Similarly, Balachandra Rajan, "*Lycidas*," in Patrides, ed., *Milton's "Lycidas*, "275: "The false surmise is not only that there is no laureate hearse; it is also the assumption that absorption in a ritual, however ardent, can serve to protect one against the assault of reality."

12. John Calvin, *Institutes of the Christian Religion*, trans. F. L. Battles, ed. John T. McNeill, Library of Christian Classics (Philadelphia: Westminster, 1960), 21:1016–19.

13. Ibid., 1035.

14. Ibid., 1051, 1054–55.

15. Cf. *De Doctrina*, I.32: "The administration of discipline is called '*the power of the keys.*' This power is not committed only to Peter or to any particular pastor in his name, but to every particular church as a totality, however few its members: Matt. xvi.19: *I will give to you the keys of the kingdom of heaven . . .* (Yale Prose, 6:609).

16. The "inherent improbability" of Milton's pastoral fiction, Johnson argues, "always forces dissatisfaction on the mind." *Lives of the English Poets* (London: Dent, 1968), 1:96. The dissatisfaction, however, is felt by the monodist as well, especially after the pilot's speech implies an alternative mode of pastoral as nurturing admonishment, as I discuss above.

17. Cited in *The Poems of John Milton*, ed. John Carey and Alastair Fowler (New York: Norton, 1972), 244.

18. Bk. XI, line 8, in Ovid, *Metamorphoses*, Loeb Classical Library (Cambridge: Harvard University Press, 1964), 2:120–21. Further references and their translations in the Loeb edition are cited parenthetically by book and line.

19. William D. Riggs also cites the "works of faith" passage in *De Doctrina*. He sees the Christian regeneration of the singer in the poem as "creative action, a work of faith emanating from a regenerate spirit ingrafted in Christ." By the end of the poem, the singer "has, finally, accomplished an active, 'eager' work of faith, which in turn anticipates new action." "The Plant of Fame in *Lycidas*," *Milton Studies* 4 (1972): 159–60.

We might compare Milton's view of the old covenant as one of works, the new as one of grace in his later poetry. In "Milton and Covenant: The Christian View of Old Testament Theology," John T. Shawcross summarizes the agon of Milton's Samson in these terms:

> Samson consistently argues for his fulfilling of God's purposes by works . . . but it is not until inward spirit has wiped away pride that he can achieve one great act of deliverance (line 1389), which represents faith and obedience. . . . In complement to *Paradise Regain'd*, where the New Covenant is developed and contrasted with the Old, *Samson Agonistes* shows how the concept of the covenant as one of works is false.

In *Milton and the Scriptural Tradition: The Bible into Poetry*, ed. James H. Sims and Leland Ryken (Columbia: University of Missouri Press, 1984), 186.

20. Johnson, *Lives*, 1:96.

CHAPTER 2. LOVE, DEATH, AND THE COMMUNION OF SAINTS

1. Elizabeth Hill, "A Dream in the Long Valley: Some Psychological Aspects of Milton's Last Sonnet," *Greyfriar* 26 (1985): 11.

2. Marilyn L. Williamson, "A Reading of Milton's Twenty-Third Sonnet," *Milton Studies* 4 (1972): 146–48.

3. Dixon Fiske, "The Theme of Purification in Milton's Sonnet XXIII," *Milton Studies* 8 (1975): 154, 158–61.

4. Kurt Heinzelman, "'Cold Consolation': The Art of Milton's Last Sonnet," *Milton Studies* 10 (1977): 114, 122.

5. When Freud discusses the paradoxical nature of dream wishes in his classic, *The Interpretation of Dreams*, he implicitly describes a complex ego-psychology influencing wishes and censorship, i.e., a desire for something followed by a desire to control the first impulse. *The Basic Writings of Sigmund Freud*, trans. and ed. A. A. Brill (New York: Modern Library, 1938), 224–25.

6. Satan, of course, is the paramount egoist of *Paradise Lost*. Nonetheless, if we consider one sinful consequence of egoism is the insistence on reducing the world and time to a centrality of self, then Adam's long lament in book X is suffused with egoism:

> O miserable of happie! is this the end
> Of this new glorious World, and mee so late
> The Glory of that Glory. . . .

(lines 720–22)

Here Adam tries to exculpate by force of ego: "Did I request, thee, Maker, from my Clay / To mould me Man" (lines 743–44); later he would nearly foreclose repentance by an egoistic theology of sin:

> all my evasions vain
> And reasonings, though through Mazes, lead me still
> But to my own conviction: first and last
> On mee, mee only, as the sourse and spring
> Of all corruption, all the blame lights due.

(lines 829–33)

In this context, self-loathing can also be a kind of selfishness. Happily for Adam, his egocentrism is countered by Eve's love, and by her sharing a more rational theology of forgiveness and renovation. For her, the serpent's role in sin is seen as important too (line 162). Her own drifting toward self-loathing and notions of suicide (lines 966–1006) finally provokes Adam to articulate some "better hopes" (1011) and to remember the prophecy of "Part of our Sentence, that thy Seed shall bruise / The Serpents head" (lines 1031–32). This conclusion is closer to the reality informing the narrator's declaration of causality in the first book of the poem: "Who first seduc'd them to that foul revolt? / Th'infernal Serpent; he it was . . . (lines 33–34).

7. William Kerrigan, "The Heretical Milton: From Assumption to Mortalism," *English Literary Renaissance* 5 (1975): 147:

> Proponents of the heresy [of mortalism], however, were able to reinstate the lost consolation of immediate immortality. . . . There is no true postponement of immor-

tality, since time is an attribute of perception and a measure of motion. Milton agreed. . . . One dies into timelessness and instantaneously one rises, glorified for judgment. This formulation displays a submerged continuity between Milton's youthful interest in assumption and his mature allegiance to mortalism. . . . While mortalism could not rescue the body from decay, those terrors were solely for the living. The dead, passing out of time, experience neither division nor dissolution. There was unexpected mercy in the strict justice of God.

In *Paradise Lost*, Adam, suffering from an "evil Conscience" (X.849) after his sin, reasons, "All of me then shall die" (X.792), which seems consistent with mortalist doctrine. C. A. Patrides, however, has noted that Adam's soliloquy is filled with a number of speculations about death and need not be taken as clearly mortalist. The doctrine was controversial but nonetheless widely held among Protestants and some Catholics, Patrides adds, citing Sir Thomas Browne, Kenelm Digby, Richard Overton, Hobbes, and Luther as adherents. C. A. Patrides, *Milton and the Christian Tradition* (Oxford: Clarendon Press, 1966), 266.

    8. Euripides, *Alcestis*, trans. Richmond Lattimore, in *The Complete Greek Tragedies*, ed. David Grene and Richmond Lattimore (Chicago: University of Chicago Press, 1955), 3:6–64, lines 1145–46. Further references are by line numbers cited parenthetically.

    9. See Heinzelman, "Cold Consolation," 114, on the "resemblance-making power of the poet" in the sonnet as the temptation of narcissism.

    10. Quoted in Richard Hooker, *Of the Laws of Ecclesiastical Polity* (London and New York: Everyman's Library, 1965), 2:400–401.

    11. Ibid., 2:399.

    12. Ibid.

    13. See also Fiske, "Theme of Purification," 154.

    Anthony Low has argued that the sonnet refers to Katherine Woodcock rather than to Mary Powell because it does not allude to "churching" at all. "Purification in the old Law," accordingly, "means just that ancient Jewish ceremony, not contemporary and erroneous Christian ceremony," which would be inappropriate to "thoughts of love and loss." The theory that the sonnet refers to Mary Powell because of a "churching" allusion is therefore wrong, even though conclusive evidence for Katherine Woodcock is lacking. "Milton's Last Sonnet," *Milton Quarterly* 9 (1975): 81.

    14. Hooker, *Ecclesiastical Polity,* 2:404.

    15. Ibid.

    16. Paul Ricoeur, *The Symbolism of Evil*, trans. Emerson Buchanan (Boston: Beacon Press, 1969), 8–10.

    17. Ibid., 28–31.

    18. Ibid., 43–44.

    19. Ibid., 25.

    20. Ibid., 51–62.

    21. Georgia Christopher has also noticed the pun:

Here "Seal" suggests the sexual imagery that John Donne favored as well as an inversion of Calvin's Communion, in which the visible analogy to God's verbal Promise was termed a "seal." Adam's lascivious onslaught upon Eve, whose virginal allure seems miraculously restored, provides a visible analogy to (and metonymy of) the violation of God's command, a deed characterized as a defloration.

Her point overall is that Milton develops the "sacramental" nature of the inspired word and draws from Reformation opposition to visual sacramentalism. *Milton and the Science of the Saints* (Princeton: Princeton University Press, 1982), 162.

22. The church discipline of Milton's marriages varied with the demands of the times. The record of Milton's marriage to Mary Powell in 1642 has never been found, but presumably the clergyman and the rite were of the established church. Milton's second marriage, to Katherine Woodcock in 1656 (the candidate for the saint favored by most commentators on the sonnet) was performed in the Guildhall by Sir John Dethicke, an alderman and justice of the peace. Civil marriages were then required, and the practice was supported by Milton (see Parker, *Milton: A Biography*, 2:1053). His marriage to Elizabeth Minshull in 1663 was probably performed by Robert Gell, the rector of St. Mary Aldermary, who had been a fellow of Christ's College, Cambridge during Milton's enrollment (ibid., 583). Gell, as Christopher Hill and others have noted, was once associated with the Family of Love sect (Familists) but then became a conforming minister of the established church during the Restoration (Hill, *Milton and the English Revolution*, 34). Hence, it is possible that of Milton's three marriage ceremonies only the second was performed independently and without the authority of the prayer book. This circumstance, if it is correct, would perhaps complement the attitude of the sonnet speaker in his placing the saint beyond mythographic and legalistic textual frames.

CHAPTER 3. SAD FAITH AND THE SOLITARY WAY

1. Instances of particular "devout affections" (trust, hope, fear, gratitude, patience, humility, obedience) in the poems are discussed in Michael E. Travers, *The Devotional Experience in the Poetry of John Milton* (Lewiston, N.Y.: Mellen, 1987). The terms are from *De Doctrina,* II.3, "Of the Virtues Which Are Related to Our Worship of God" (Yale Prose, 6:656).

"Affections" as the terms or vocabulary of a moral psychology are of course important in much Puritan theology, especially in the doctrine of repentance and conversion. Cf. William Fenner, *A Treatise of the Affections; or the Soules Pulse* (London, 1642): "Religion is more in the affections of the soul than in the effects and operations." Quoted in Charles Lloyd Cohen, *God's Caress: The Psychology of Puritan Religious Experience* (New York and Oxford: Oxford University Press, 1986), 119.

2. Hill, *Milton and the English Revolution*, 394–95.

3. Boyd Berry, *Process of Speech: Puritan Religious Writing and Paradise Lost* (Baltimore: Johns Hopkins University Press, 1976).

4. Lieb, *Poetics of the Holy*, 38–39.

5. For the antisabbatarian poet, Berry points out, "the true Christian is not bound by space or time in his worship which should flow in unpremeditated strains to the glory of the eternal Sabbath" (*Process of Speech,* 99).

On the typological allusion to Christ's fruitful relationship with the church figured by the hierarchic and loving union of Adam and Eve, see Mary Ruth Brown, "*Paradise Lost* and John 15: Eve, the Branch, and the Church," *Milton Quarterly* 20 (1986): 127–31. Ann Kibbey, however, has found a problematic significance in the "living icons" associated with Puritan sanctification generally and with the figure of the mystical body, a figure at times associated with threats to civil liberty. *The Interpretation of Material Shapes in Puritanism: A Study of Rhetoric, Prejudice, and Violence* (New York and Cambridge: Cambridge University Press, 1986), 133.

It might be noted that in seventeenth-century contexts "sad" can mean gravely strong and valiant as well as sorrowful and dismal, mature and sober as well as morose, as the *Oxford English Dictionary* illustrates. The adjective may therefore be consistent with a demeanor of empowerment as well as of tragic loss for Adam and Eve.

6. Reid Barbour has argued that Eve's earlier, fearful dream of the forbidden fruit in the bower (*P.L.,* V.28–94) is an implicit caution against gazing on liturgical objects and forms. Her "Laudian gaze on the sacred object, the tree and its fruits," expresses Milton's belief that "freedom is always compromised by its search for outer forms." However, Adam's defining her dream (*P.L,* V.95–121) is the result of "a gendered hierarchy," and, ironically, the spontaneous prayer after the dream becomes "an externalized, formal answer to Eve's demonic flights of fancy." "Liturgy and Dreams in Seventeenth-Century England," *Modern Philology* 88 (1991): 240–41.

To be sure, a hierarchy of gender partly defines the union of Adam and Eve in the poem both before and after the fall. Eve's second, authoritative dream in book XII, however, complements (or perhaps makes redundant) Adam's didacticism. Eve still defers to Adam, but he is "Well-pleas'd" rather than threatened by her insight (*P.L,* XII.625). The prophetic role of women in Congregationalism is perhaps alluded to here, or at least the tendency among Independents to de-emphasize the role of the minister in order to encourage a unanimity of faith in the Pauline sense of different gifts for different members of the church body. Of course, elders and prophets were predominately male, and in some congregations the role of women did not even include their questioning of prophets during this part of the service (see Cotton, *Doctrine of the Church*, 6). Nonetheless, some women participated in congregational study groups analyzing sermons and in some congregations could exercise an informal leadership. The celebrated Anne Hutchinson in Massachusetts could count Milton's colleague, Sir Henry Vane, among her followers during his brief tenure as governor of the colony in 1636. That she was persecuted for heresy (and presumably for undermining the hierarchy of gender in church leadership) and that her study groups included men as well as women would, for some, be evidence of her spiritual authority. See Cohen, *God's Caress*, 261–70.

Whatever the actual extent of the role of women in Independency, some detractors would regard their presumed authority as proof of a monstrous imbalance throughout such congregations. The well-known Presbyterian, John Vicars, for instance, ridicules congregations of the saints inclusively when addressing his dissenting brethren in *The Picture of Independency* (London, 1645), 9–10:

By this means also making and esteeming every particular *Congregation*, yea every *particular Saint* of yours (as ye cal them) a true and *entire Church*, as Mr. D. one of your *Independent Brethren* holds, and publickly teaches; to every of whom equally, ye say, the *Keyes belong*, (and I think, by this rule, to the *Women-Saints* as well as to the *Men-Saints*) not being subject to any *appeale or coercive-power* other than your own.

7. The association of idolatrous worship with degenerate sexuality is of course scriptural (Gal. 5:19–20, Acts 15:20, and Rev. 2. 14, for example). Adam's description of Eve's loss of innocence defines her behavior as also a kind of sexual wantonness, an encounter marring the right order of creation rather than affirming the norms of procreation. The rhetorical figure of fornication is in turn relatable to the insubordinate egoism of an "idolater" in a broader, cultural sense of the term, as Milton explains in *Tetrachordon*:

For the language of Scripture signifies by fornication . . . not only the trespas of body nor perhaps that between married persons, unless in a degree or quality as shameles as the *Bordello*, but signifies also any notable disobedience, or intractable cariage of the wife to the husband. . . . Secondly signifies the apparent alienation of mind not to idolatry, (which may seem to answer the act of adultery) but farre on this side, to any point of will worship, though to the true God; some times it notes the love of earthly things, or worldly pleasures though on a right beleever, some times the least suspicion of unwitting idolatry. (Yale Prose, 2:672)

The sexual episode that is narratively described as "the Seal" of Adam and Eve's "mutual guilt," and the "solace of thir sin" (*P.L.*, IX.1043–44) is also a debased communion, one alluding to a sacramental "seal," as Georgia Christopher has observed in *Milton and the Science of the Saints*, 162 (and as noted above in my discussion of the Twenty-Third Sonnet). Perhaps, too, Adam's rude possessing of his wife ("Her hand he seis'd" [*P.L.*, IX.1037]) and her own "contagious Fire" (IX.1036) suggest the carnal disorders of the church.

8. John C. Ulreich maintains that even though Milton repudiates sacramentalism in the Catholic sense in *De Doctrina*, he does positively depict a kind of sacramentalism in *Paradise Lost*, especially the doctrine of "sacramental participation" that "the essence of a sacrament is *communion* with Christ." This participation is cognitive, "a conscious act of imagination" by the believer, and draws on material elements in order to substantiate the invisible church. "Milton on the Eucharist: Some Second Thoughts About Sacramentalism," in *Milton and the Middle Ages*, ed. John Mulryan (Lewisburg, Pa.: Bucknell University Press, 1982), 45, 49.

9. Cf. Thomas Gataker, *Noah His Obedience* (London, 1623), 85: "Noah in making of his *Arke* did, as *Basil* speaketh, *preach without preaching*. Every stroke that was strucke, every nail that was driven in the framing of it, was a *fore-telling of the Floud*, and a *reall* Sermon of repentance."

Chapter 4. The Unobserved Kingdom

1. The theological significance of a mystical kingdom in *Paradise Regain'd* has been generally explained by Fixler, *Milton and the Kingdoms of God*, and by Barbara Lewalski, *Milton's Brief Epic: The Genre, Meaning, and Art of "Paradise Regained"* (Providence, R.I.: Brown University Press, 1966). The poem as an "internalized epic" of ego psychology (one influencing the subjective epics of the nineteenth-century romantics) has been discussed by Stuart Curran, "The Mental Pinnacle: *Paradise Regained* and the Romantic Four-Book Epic," in *Calm of Mind: Tercentenary Essays on "Paradise Regained" and "Samson Agonistes" in Honor of John S. Diekhoff*, ed. Joseph Wittreich (Cleveland: Case Western Reserve University, 1971), 133–62.

In *The Empty Garden: The Subject of Late Milton* (Pittsburgh: University of Pittsburgh Press, 1992), 352, Ashraf H. A. Rushdy comments, "Milton's representation of Jesus in the wilderness is also a figural representation of the beginnings of the collective church— in fact of its metaphorical head at the outset of its mission." Rushdy's emphasis is on the process of the Son gaining self-knowledge in the poem and on how the development of the inward man is central to Milton's general theory of culture.

2. Cf. Christopher, *Milton and the Science of the Saints*, 105, on how Calvin's requirements concerning mastery of the catechism "began to eclipse baptism as the rite of initiation into the Kingdom of God."

3. See John T. Shawcross, *Paradise Regain'd: Worthy T'Have Not Remain'd So Long Unsung* (Pittsburgh: Duquesne University Press, 1988), 39–40, on this recognition and echo as an expression of prior knowledge on the part of the Son and as a dramatic anagnorisis for Satan. In the poem, the hero does not experience a conventional recognition of identity, at least not after book I, Shawcross explains. Rather, the antagonist has this recognition. *Paradise Regain'd*, then, "works constantly on reversal of expectation." Later, the Son does not suddenly achieve divine identity when presented with Satan's dilemma on the Temple spire; because of his faith, he does not face this as a dilemma.

4. See Shawcross, *Paradise Regain'd*, 63–69. The Son's mature identity as a man is mythically implied by his leaving the mother-child relationship, then by "taking on the energy of the Father." The form of his life, "the pattern of meekness" by which the Father's energy is conveyed in the world, derives from the mother, however. The Son's return to his mother's house at the end of the poem suggests both "a metaphoric return to the womb (a death symbol)" and the completion of form. The Son, moreover, "represents the oneness of Man and Woman, and *Paradise Regain'd* proclaims that Mankind's place of rest will be attained only by the symbolic Adam and Eve within us all going forth hand in hand." This internal, self-reliant identity is both heroic achievement and spiritual model.

On the identity of Jesus as one conditioned by the mother and private life, in contrast to Samson's identity in Milton's dramatic poem, see Rushdy, *Empty Garden,* 328. See also Christopher, *Milton and the Science of the Saints,* 224, on the Son's "self abnegation" (as opposed to the temptation of "self-mastery") leading to the Spirit's guidance. In turn, the gift of the Spirit is to be shared with all believers, and the poem "attempts no metaphysical definition of the incarnate Christ nor even provides any clear line of demarcation between the Messiah and the ordinary Christian."

5. In regarding baptism as a seal of prior grace and of divine forgiveness, and as "a sign of our death and resurrection with Christ," *De Doctrina* is certainly within the broadest margins of Protestantism. By adding that it is also a seal of "sanctification," i.e., of the appropriate attitude for living one's faith, and by arguing for adult baptism as that which rightly requires "conditions" of rationality and cognitive faith, the treatise supports a narrower, more radical discipline (Yale Prose, 6:548). Milton seems to favor the discipline of adult baptism in other texts undoubtedly his, as Hill, "Professor William B. Hunter, Bishop Burgess, and John Milton," points out. Hill cites passages in *Considerations Touching the Likeliest Means to Remove Hirelings Out of the Church* (Yale Prose, 7:248), *Of Reformation* (Yale Prose, 1:555–56), and *The Doctrine and Discipline of Divorce* (Yale Prose, 2:231, 302), among others. Hill's point here, of course, is that Milton must therefore be the author of *De Doctrina*.

Perhaps clouding the issue is the actual practice of the Milton household. The baptismal records of at least two of Milton's five children exist and are dated from their infancies—Mary in 1648 and Deborah in 1652—as cited in Parker, *Milton: A Biography*, 1:340, 411. To be sure, Puritans did not uniformly oppose infant baptism. Rather, the "antipaedobaptist" position was the inevitable extension of Separatist ecclesiology if not always the prevailing practice among Separatists and Independents. See Brachlow, *Communion of Saints*, 150–56.

6. If *Paradise Regain'd* was originally intended to be a drama or dramatic poem like *Samson Agonistes*, as Shawcross (*Paradise Regain'd,* 29–44), Parker (*Milton: A Biography*, 2:1139), and others believe, then perhaps the Son's account of the baptism (first conceived as a soliloquy, or monologue heard by a chorus) could be analogous to the personal testimonies leading to full church membership in Puritan congregations. The Son's recalling

such heavenly signs, along with John's and Mary's autobiographical accounts of experiencing grace and divine authority, is in a sense a paradigm for the informal liturgy of membership. Radical congregations varied in the degrees of spiritual autobiography encouraged or required of members, but all seem to have agreed that a Christian's faith should be demonstrated by actualizations and narratives of some kind, rather than by mere recitations of the creed and general professions of faith such as found in the prayer book of the established church. "Effectual confession, as the church may well approve of," in Robert Parker's words, is continuous with "good signs of regeneration" (quoted in Brachlow, *Communion of Saints,* 125). The once Independent, John Rogers, collected and published over forty such testimonies from his own Dublin congregation in *A Tabernacle for the Sun* (1653). See John Taylor, "Some Seventeenth-Century Testimonies," *Transactions of the Congregational Historical Society* 16 (1949–51): 64–77, for a brief discussion of Rogers's book.

7. Lewalski, *Milton's Brief Epic,* 211, comments on Satan's travesty of the good shepherd in the episode, and concludes, "Christ here implies that his proper sustenance is the Word of God. . . . In his role as prophet, then, Christ, the True Bread that has come down from heaven, the Incarnate Word," overturns Satan's false teachings.

8. Cf. Shawcross, *Paradise Regain'd,* 63, on the "form" of the Son's public ministry as maternally influenced. Beyond this influence, the Son's conceptual formulations of "All his great work to come" seem to be inspired by a nurturing attribute of the Spirit, divinity both impregnating and brooding with a simultaneously masculine and feminine energy.

9. Cf. Lewalski, *Milton's Brief Epic,* 217, on the suggestions of a Catholic cathedral and the idolatry of the mass in the scene. Here the Son rejects a "false priesthood" and claims "the freedom from ceremonial restriction which is the mark of the new covenant."

10. The figurative and mystical associations of the Son's body standing on (and relegating) the Temple, an image of two contrasting temples, are also present in Milton's prose. O'Keeffe, *Milton and the Pauline Tradition,* 246–47, cites *The Reason of Church Government,* where Milton uses "the temple-body image" not simply as a metaphor of purity but as a formulation of "an inner awareness of worship" in the architecture of the new covenant.

11. Patient, courageous standing is of course a common reformist posture or figure in Congregational worship and Protestant church history. In *Paradise Lost,* Adam and Eve pray in various postures—standing (XI.1), kneeling (XI.148–49), and prostrate (X.1098–1100). We can also compare, however, the concluding, triumphant image of Sonnet XIX, a miniature psychomachia, where standing implies a fully informed sanctification, a position enabling right worship and discipline in the community of the faithful. In the sonnet, the adversary is a more strictly internalized ethic of works, an enemy nonetheless who tempts by framing identity in terms of ambitions fulfilled or frustrated. This irksome, if not fiendish, egoism is defeated by "patience" voicing the Gospel's exhortation to bear the Lord's easy yoke:

> Doth God exact day labour, light deny'd,
> I fondly ask; but patience to prevent
> That murmur, soon replies, God doth not need
> Either man's work or his own gifts, who best
> Bear his mild yoak, they serve him best, his State
> Is Kingly. Thousands at his bidding speed
> And post o're Land and Ocean without rest:
> They also serve who only stand and wait.

(lines 7–14)

Cf. Lieb, *Poetics of the Holy,* 298–99, and Hill, *Milton and the English Revolution,* 419.

12. See *De Doctrina,* I.28 (Yale Prose, 6:548).

13. See Lewalski, *Milton's Brief Epic,* 271–72, on how these lines "greatly modify" the Son's original severity by their sense of the "peaceful restoration of the lost ones" in God's providential time. The lines also allude to the millennial kingdom of Isaiah and to the eventually peaceful kingdom of the church.

14. Vane, *The Face of the Times* (London, 1662), 73, paraphrases Luke 17:21 and emphasizes a new opportunity for spiritual development among outcast Christians:

> This Kingdom of Christ is capable of substituting and being managed inwardly, in the minds of his People, in a hidden state, concealed from the eye of the world; By the Power thereof, the inward senses or eyes of the mind are opened and awakened, to the drawing them upward to a Heavenly converse, catching and carrying up the Soul to the Throne of God, and to the knowledge of the Life which is hid, with Christ, in God. Those that are in this Kingdom, and in whom the Power of it is, are fitted to flye with the Church into the Wildernesse and to continue in such a solitary, dispersed, desolate condition, till God calls them out of it.

Some of Vane's readers probably took his idea of Christ's kingdom concealed to be the Puritan cause as a Church Militant shifted to underground revolution or to subversion of the restored monarchy. The pamphlet was published with the following title, which may anticipate some of the political allusions of Milton's great poems a few years later: *An Epistle General to the Mystical Body of Christ on Earth, Published with the Face of the Times Wherein is Discovered . . . the Enmity and Contest, between the Seed of the Woman and the Seed of the Serpent.*

Hill, *Milton and the English Revolution,* 415, also notices a parallel with Vane's figure of the kingdom of Christ in the wilderness.

15. While the conclusion of the poem alludes to the nurturing aspect of true religion and, I believe, of the body of the unspoiled church, it might be noted that Milton did not like the term "mother church." In what he admits is the "rougher accent," or adversarial rhetoric, of *Animadversions upon the Remonstrant's Defence Against Smectymnuus* (1641), he objects to the way "crafty" Anglican bishops have appropriated such a papastical term and used it to cow English Protestants. In this same context, he mocks the prelatical usage of "invisible church," as a similar attempt to obscure the fecklessness of prelates' spiritual authority. Rather, he declares, the terms themselves have no incantatory power:

> What should we doe or say to this *Remonstrant*? that by his idle, and shallow reasonings seemes to have been conversant in no Divinity, but that which is colourable to uphold Bishopricks. Wee acknowledge, and beleeve the Catholick reformed Church, and if any man be dispos's to use a trope or figure, as Saint *Paul* once did in calling her the common Mother of us all, let him doe as his owne rethorick shall perswade him. (Yale Prose, 1:727)

Cf. Anthony Low, *The Reinvention of Love: Poetry, Politics and Culture from Sidney to Milton* (Cambridge: Cambridge University Press, 1993), 167. Low takes this passage as uncompromising: "So much for the Church's motherhood. And so much for the concept of a true, 'invisible' Church that transcended the imperfections of churches in this world." Moreover, Milton's seemingly positive citations of the marriage trope of Christ as husband of the church in *The Reason of Church Government* are, in Low's view, merely "perfunctory"

(239 n. 17). Instead, Low argues, Milton's religious individualism promulgates a model of love without institutional and societal mediation, and without the figures of such mediation.

CHAPTER 5. TRUE RELIGION AND TRAGEDY

1. See Francis Fergusson, *The Idea of a Theatre* (Princeton: Princeton University Press, 1968), 33.

2. Barbara Lewalski has commented on redemptive allusions in neoclassical biblical tragedy as influences on *Paradise Lost*. She cites Grotius's *Adamus Exul* (1601) and Della Salandra's *Adam Caduto* (1647). *"Paradise Lost" and the Rhetoric of Literary Forms* (Princeton: Princeton University Press, 1985), 222–23.

3. Thomas B. Stroup, *Religious Rite and Ceremony in Milton's Poetry* (Lexington: University Press of Kentucky, 1968), 57–62.

4. Sherman H. Hawkins, "Samson's Catharsis," *Milton Studies* 2 (1970): 226–27.

5. Lieb, *Poetics of the Holy*, 77.

6. Mary Ann Radzinowicz, *Toward "Samson Agonistes": The Growth of Milton's Mind* (Princeton: Princeton University Press, 1978), 363.

7. Joseph Wittreich, *Interpreting "Samson Agonistes"* (Princeton: Princeton University Press, 1986), 363–64.

8. Joan S. Bennet, *Reviving Liberty: Radical Christian Humanism in Milton's Great Poems* (Cambridge: Harvard University Press, 1989), 120–24.

9. Ernest B. Gilman, *Iconoclasm and Poetry in the English Reformation* (Chicago: University of Chicago Press, 1986), 171–75.

10. Rushdy, *Empty Garden*, 293.

11. Bennet, *Reviving Liberty*, 132.

12. Calvin, *Institutes*, 397. Cf. *De Doctrina*, II.7 (Yale Prose, 6:351–55, 704–15).

13. *Poems of John Milton*, ed. Carey and Fowler, 996–97. Cf. above, "Sad Faith and the Solitary Way," 70.

14. William G. Madsen, *From Shadowy Types to Truth* (New Haven: Yale University Press, 1968), 111.

15. Cf. Milton's *Artis Logicae* (Yale Prose VIII, 232) and *Tetrachordon* (Yale Prose, 2:608), where the same Aristotelian definition is used.

16. Bennet, *Reviving Liberty*, 120–24.

17. Wittreich, *Interpreting "Samson Agonistes,"* 194–95, cites several Cromwellian apologists writing in the 1640s who saw Samson's destruction of the Philistine temple as exalting the common believer and foretelling the ruin of Romish and Anglican church government.

Cf. Christopher Hill, *The Experience of Defeat: Milton and Some Contemporaries* (New York: Viking, 1984), 314–15, on why Milton departs from Judges in having the common people survive: "I can see no reason for these innovations of Milton's except to condemn the clergy and aristocracy whom he regarded as the principal enemies of God in restoration England: and perhaps to show that he now had more hope of 'the vulgar' responding to a purged and purified leadership than when he wrote *Paradise Regained*."

18. Ricki Heller, "Opposites of Wifehood: Eve and Dalila," *Milton Studies* 24 (1988): 187–202.

19. Cf. *A Treatise of Civil Power*:

That the inward man is nothing els but the inward part of man, his understanding and his will, and that his actions thence proceeding, yet not simply thence but from the work of divine grace upon them, are the whole matter of religion under the gospel, will appeer planely by considering what that religion is; whence we shall perceive yet more planely that it cannot be forc'd. What euangelic religion is, is told in two words, faith and charitie; or beleef and practise. (Yale Prose, 7:255)

20. On this sense of parable, see John D. Crosson, *The Dark Interval: Towards a Theology of Story* (Niles, Ill.: Argus Communications, 1975), 123.

Works Cited

Achinstein, Sharon. *Milton and the Revolutionary Reader*. Princeton: Princeton University Press, 1994.

Baillie, Robert. *A Dissuasive from the Errours of the Time*. London, 1645.

Baker, Stewart A. "Milton's Uncouth Swain." *Milton Studies* 3 (1971): 38–43.

Barbour, Reid. "Liturgy and Dreams in Seventeenth-Century England." *Modern Philology* 88, no. 3 (February 1991).

Barker, Arthur E. *Milton and the Puritan Dilemma*. Toronto: University of Toronto Press, 1942.

Bennet, Joan S. *Reviving Liberty: Radical Christian Humanism in Milton's Great Poems*. Cambridge: Harvard University Press, 1989.

Berry, Boyd. *Process of Speech: Puritan Religious Writing and "Paradise Lost."* Baltimore: The Johns Hopkins University Press, 1976.

Brachlow, Stephen. *The Communion of Saints: Radical Puritan and Separatist Ecclesiology, 1570–1625*. Oxford: Oxford University Press, 1988.

Brown, Mary Ruth. "*Paradise Lost* and John 15: Eve, the Branch, and the Church." *Milton Quarterly* 20 (1986): 127–31.

Burton, Henry. *A Vindication of Churches Commonly Called Independent*. London, 1644.

Calvin, John. *Institutes of the Christian Religion*. Translated by F. L. Battles. Edited by John T. McNeill. Vol. 21, Library of Christian Classics. Philadelphia: Westminster, 1960.

Christopher, Georgia B. *Milton and the Science of the Saints*. Princeton: Princeton University Press, 1982.

Cohen, Charles Lloyd. *God's Caress: The Psychology of Puritan Religious Experience*. New York: Oxford University Press, 1986.

Cotton, John. *The Doctrine of the Church*. London, 1644.

Crossan, John D. *The Dark Interval: Towards a Theology of Story*. Niles, Ill.: Argus Communications, 1975.

Curran, Stuart. "The Mental Pinnacle: *Paradise Regained* and the Romantic Four-Book Epic." In *Calm of Mind: Tercentenary Essays on "Paradise Regained" and "Samson*

Agonistes" in Honor of John S. Diekhoff, edited by Joseph Wittreich, 133–62. Cleveland: The Press of Case Western Reserve University, 1971.

Donne, John. *The Complete Poetry of John Donne*. Edited by John T. Shawcross. New York: Anchor Books, 1967.

Dulles, Avery. "Church Membership." In *The Encyclopedia of Religion*, edited by Mircea Eliade, 3:486–88. New York: Macmillan, 1987.

Euripides. *Alcestis*. In *The Complete Greek Tragedies*, translated by Richmond Lattimore, edited by David Grene and Richmond Lattimore, 3:6-64. Chicago: University of Chicago Press, 1955.

Fergusson, Francis. *The Idea of a Theatre*. Princeton: Princeton University Press, 1968.

Fish, Stanley. "*Lycidas:* A Poem Finally Anonymous." In *Milton's "Lycidas": The Tradition and the Poem*, edited by C. A. Patrides, 322–40. Columbia: University of Missouri Press, 1983.

Fiske, Dixon. "The Theme of Purification in Milton's Sonnet XXIII." *Milton Studies* 8 (1975): 149–63.

Fixler, Michael. "Ecclesiology." In *A Milton Encyclopedia*, edited by William B. Hunter Jr., et al., 2:190–203. Lewisburg, Pa.: Bucknell University Press, 1978.

———. *Milton and the Kingdoms of God*. Chicago: Northwestern University Press, 1964.

Freud, Sigmund. *The Interpretation of Dreams*. In *The Basic Writings of Sigmund Freud*, translated and edited by A. A. Brill, 181–549. New York: The Modern Library, 1938.

Friedman, Donald M. "*Lycidas:* The Swain's Paideia." In *Milton's "Lycidas": The Tradition and the Poem*, edited by C. A. Patrides, 281–302. Columbia: University of Missouri Press, 1983.

Gataker, Thomas. *Noah His Obedience*. In *Two Sermons*. London, 1623.

Gilman, Ernest B. *Iconoclasm and Poetry in the English Reformation*. Chicago: University of Chicago Press, 1986.

Grotius, Hugo. *Hugo Grotius His Sophompaneos, or Ioseph. A Tragedy*. Translated by Francis Goldsmith, Esq. London, 1652.

Hawkins, Sherman H. "Samson's Catharsis." *Milton Studies* 2 (1970): 211–30.

Heinzelman, Kurt. "'Cold Consolation': The Art of Milton's Last Sonnet." *Milton Studies* 10 (1977): 111–25.

Heller, Ricki. "Opposites of Wifehood: Eve and Dalila." *Milton Studies* 24 (1988): 187–202.

Henry, N. H. *The True Wayfaring Christian: Studies in Milton's Puritanism*. New York: Peter Lang, 1987.

———. "Who Meant License When They Cried Liberty." *Modern Language Notes* 66 (1951): 509–13.

Hill, Christopher. *The Experience of Defeat: Milton and Some Contemporaries*. New York: Viking, 1984.

———. *Milton and the English Revolution*. New York: Viking, 1977.

———. "Professor William B. Hunter, Bishop Burgess, and John Milton." *Studies in English Literature* 34 (1994): 165–93.

Hill, Elizabeth. "A Dream in the Long Valley: Some Psychological Aspects of Milton's Last Sonnet." *Greyfriar* 26 (1985): 3–13.

Honeygosky, Stephen R. *Milton's House of God: The Invisible and Visible Church*. Columbia: University of Missouri Press, 1993.

Hooker, Richard. *Of the Laws of Ecclesiastical Polity*. Vol. 2. London and New York: Everyman's Library, 1965.

Hunter, William B. "Animadversions upon the Remonstrants' Defenses against Burgess and Hunter." *Studies in English Literature* 34 (1994): 165–93.

———. "Milton Translates the Psalms." *Philological Quarterly* 40 (1961): 485–94.

———. "The Provenance of the *Christian Doctrine*." *Studies in English Literature* 32 (1992): 129–42, 163–66.

———. "The Provenance of the *Christian Doctrine:* Addenda from the Bishop of Salisbury." *Studies in English Literature* 33 (1993): 191–207.

Hyman, Lawrence W. *The Quarrel Within: Art and Morality in Milton's Poetry*. Port Washington, N.Y.: Kennikat Press, 1972.

Johnson, Samuel. *Lives of the English Poets*. London: Dent, 1968.

Kerrigan, William. "The Heretical Milton: From Assumption to Mortalism." *English Literary Renaissance* 5 (1975): 125–66.

———. *The Prophetic Milton*. Charlottesville: University Press of Virginia, 1974.

Kibbey, Ann. *The Interpretation of Material Shapes in Puritanism: A Study of Rhetoric, Prejudice, and Violence*. New York: Cambridge University Press, 1986.

Lawry, Jon S. *The Shadow of Heaven: Matter and Stance in Milton's Poetry*. Ithaca: Cornell University Press, 1968.

Leishman, Thomas, ed. *The Westminster Directory*. Edinburgh and London: William Blackwood and Sons, 1901.

Lewalski, Barbara Kiefer. *Milton's Brief Epic: The Genre, Meaning, and Art of "Paradise Regained."* Providence, R.I.: Brown University Press, 1966.

———. *"Paradise Lost" and the Rhetoric of Literary Forms*. Princeton: Princeton University Press, 1985.

Lieb, Michael. *Poetics of the Holy: A Reading of "Paradise Lost."* Chapel Hill: University of North Carolina Press, 1981.

———. *The Sinews of Ulysses: Form and Convention in Milton's Works*. Pittsburgh: Duquesne University Press, 1989.

Low, Anthony. "Milton's Last Sonnet." *Milton Quarterly* 9 (1975): 80–81.

———. *The Reinvention of Love: Poetry, Politics, and Culture from Sidney to Milton*. Cambridge: Cambridge University Press, 1993.

Madsen, William G. *From Shadowy Types to Truth*. New Haven: Yale University Press, 1968.

Marvell, Andrew. *Complete Poetry*. Edited by George deF. Lord. New York: The Modern Library, 1968.

Masson, David. *The Life of John Milton: Narrated in Connexion With the Political, Ecclesiastical, and Literary History of His Time*. 7 vols. 1859–94. Reprint, Gloucester, Mass.: Peter Smith, 1965.

McGuire, Maryann. *Milton's Puritan Masque*. Athens: University of Georgia Press, 1983.

McLoone, George H. *"Lycidas:* Hurled Bones and the Noble Mind of Reformed Congregations." *Milton Studies* 26 (1991): 59–80.

———. "Milton's Twenty-Third Sonnet: Love, Death, and the Mystical Body of the Church." *Milton Quarterly* 24 (1990): 8–20.

———. "'True Religion' and Tragedy: Milton's Insights in *Samson Agonistes*." *Mosaic* 28, no. 3 (1995): 1–29.

Milton, John. *The Complete Poetry of John Milton*. Edited by John T. Shawcross. New York: Anchor Books, 1971.

———. *Complete Prose Works* of John Milton. Edited by Don M. Wolfe. 8 vols. New Haven: Yale University Press, 1953–82.

———. *The Poems of John Milton*. Edited by John Carey and Alastair Fowler. New York: Norton, 1972.

O'Keeffe, Timothy J. *Milton and the Pauline Tradition: A Study of Theme and Symbolism*. Lanham, Md.: University Press of America, 1982.

Ovid. *Metamorphoses*. Loeb Classical Library. Cambridge: Harvard University Press, 1964.

Parker, William Riley. *Milton: A Biography*. 2 vols. Oxford: Clarendon, 1968.

———. *Milton's Contemporary Reputation*. Columbus: Ohio State University Press, 1940.

Patrides, C. A. *Milton and the Christian Tradition*. Oxford: Clarendon Press, 1966.

Pope, Elizabeth. *"Paradise Regained": The Tradition and the Poem*. Baltimore: The Johns Hopkins University Press, 1947.

Radzinowicz, Mary Ann. *Toward "Samson Agonistes": The Growth of Milton's Mind*. Princeton: Princeton University Press, 1978.

Rajan, Balachandra. *"Lycidas."* In *Milton's "Lycidas": The Tradition and the Poem*, edited by C. A. Patrides, 267–80. Columbia: University of Missouri Press, 1983.

Ricoeur, Paul. *The Symbolism of Evil*. Translated by Emerson Buchanan. Boston: Beacon Press, 1969.

Riggs, William D. "The Plant of Fame in *Lycidas*." *Milton Studies* 4 (1972): 151–62.

Rogers, John. *A Tabernacle for the Sun*. 1653.

Rushdy, Ashraf H. A. *The Empty Garden: The Subject of Late Milton*. Pittsburgh: University of Pittsburgh Press, 1992.

Sacks, Peter M. "Lycidas." In *John Milton: Modern Critical Views,* edited by Harold Bloom, 297–92. New York: Chelsea House, 1986.

Schreiner, Susan E. "Church." In *The Oxford Encyclopedia of the Reformation*, edited by Hans Hillerbrand, 1:323–27. London: Oxford University Press, 1996.

Shawcross, John T. "Milton and Covenant: The Christian View of Old Testament Theology." In *Milton and the Scriptural Tradition: The Bible into Poetry*, edited by James H. Sims and Leland Ryken, 160–91. Columbia: University of Missouri Press, 1984.

———. *"Paradise Regain'd": Worthy T'Have Not Remain'd So Long Unsung*. Pittsburgh: Duquesne University Press, 1988.

Spitzer, Leo. "Understanding Milton." *Hopkins Review* 4 (1951): 116–31.

Stroup, Thomas B. *Religious Rite and Ceremony in Milton's Poetry*. Lexington: University Press of Kentucky, 1968.

Taylor, John. "Some Seventeenth-Century Testimonies." *Transactions of the Congregational Historical Society* 16 (1949–51): 64–77.

Travers, Michael. *The Devotional Experience in the Poetry of John Milton*. Studies in Art and Religious Interpretation, no. 10 Lewiston, N.Y.: Mellen, 1987.

Ulreich, John C., Jr. "'And By Occasion Foretells': The Prophetic Voice in *Lycidas*." *Milton Studies* 18 (1983): 3–23.

———. "Milton on the Eucharist: Some Second Thoughts About Sacramentalism." In *Milton and the Middle Ages,* edited by John Mulryan, 32–56. Lewisburg, Pa.: Bucknell University Press, 1982.

Vane, Sir Henry. *The Face of the Times*. London, 1662.

Vicars, John. *The Picture of Independency Lively (yet Lovingly) Delineated*. London, 1645.

Williamson, Marilyn L. "A Reading of Milton's Twenty-Third Sonnet." *Milton Studies* 4 (1972): 141-49.

Wittreich, Joseph. *Interpreting "Samson Agonistes."* Princeton: Princeton University Press, 1986.

———. *Visionary Poetics: Milton's Tradition and his Legacy*. San Marino, Calif.: Huntington Library Press, 1979.

Wolfe, Don M. *Milton in the Puritan Revolution*. New York: Nelson, 1941. Reprint, Atlantic Highlands, N.J.: Humanities Press, 1963.

Yaghijian, Lucretia Bailey. "The Poet and the Church: Visible and Invisible Images of *Ecclesia* in the Early Prose and Poetry of John Milton, 1634–1645." Ann Arbor, Mich.: University Microfilms, 1976.

Index